# DECISIONS AND DISSENTS OF JUSTICE RUTH BADER GINSBURG

**Ruth Bader Ginsburg** is an associate justice of the United States Supreme Court. Appointed by President Bill Clinton and confirmed by a 96–3 vote in the Senate, she has served on the Court since August 10, 1993. Ginsburg's appointment made her just the second woman to join the Supreme Court. Previously, Ginsburg had served as a judge on the United States Court of Appeals for the District of Columbia, and was the founder of the Women's Rights Project at the American Civil Liberties Union, the founding faculty advisor of the *Women's Rights Law Reporter*, and a professor of law at Rutgers Law School and Columbia Law School. Ginsburg was born Joan Ruth Bader in Brooklyn in 1933. She holds a BA from Cornell University, was the first woman to join the *Harvard Law Review*, and holds a JD from Columbia Law School, where she also joined the law review and graduated first in her class.

**Corey Brettschneider** is a professor of political science at Brown University, where he teaches constitutional law and politics, as well as a visiting professor of law at Fordham University School of Law. He has also been a visiting professor at Harvard Law School and the University of Chicago Law School. His writing has appeared in *The New York Times*, *Politico*, and *The Washington Post*. He is the author of *The Oath and the Office: A Guide to the Constitution for Future Presidents*, two books about constitutional law and civil liberties, and numerous articles published in academic journals and law reviews. His constitutional law casebook is widely used in classrooms throughout the United States. Brettschneider holds a PhD in politics from Princeton University and a JD from Stanford Law School.

# Decisions and Dissents
## of
# JUSTICE RUTH BADER GINSBURG

## A Selection

EDITED WITH AN INTRODUCTION BY
## Corey Brettschneider

SERIES EDITOR
## Corey Brettschneider

PENGUIN BOOKS

PENGUIN BOOKS
An imprint of Penguin Random House LLC
penguinrandomhouse.com

Series introduction, volume introduction,
and selection copyright © 2020 by Corey Brettschneider
Penguin supports copyright. Copyright fuels creativity, encourages diverse voices,
promotes free speech, and creates a vibrant culture. Thank you for buying an authorized
edition of this book and for complying with copyright laws by not reproducing, scanning,
or distributing any part of it in any form without permission. You are supporting writers
and allowing Penguin to continue to publish books for every reader.

LIBRARY OF CONGRESS CATALOGING-IN-PUBLICATION DATA
Names: Ginsburg, Ruth Bader, author. | Brettschneider, Corey Lang,
editor, writer of introduction.
Title: Decisions and dissents of Justice Ruth Bader Ginsburg : a selection /
edited with an introduction by Corey Brettschneider.
Other titles: Judicial opinions. Selections
Description: New York : Penguin Books, 2020. | Series: Penguin liberty
Identifiers: LCCN 2020008191 (print) | LCCN 2020008192 (ebook) |
ISBN 9780143135111 (paperback) | ISBN 9780525506799 (ebook)
Subjects: LCSH: Dissenting opinions—United States. | Law—United States—Cases. |
LCGFT: Court decisions and opinions.
Classification: LCC KF213.G56 B74 2020 (print) | LCC KF213.G56 (ebook) |
DDC 347.73/2634—dc23
LC record available at https://lccn.loc.gov/2020008191
LC ebook record available at https://lccn.loc.gov/2020008192

Printed in the United States of America
1  3  5  7  9  10  8  6  4  2

Book design by Daniel Lagin

# Contents

## *Decisions and Dissents of*
## JUSTICE RUTH BADER GINSBURG

# Series Introduction

On November 9, 1989, the Berlin Wall fell. Two years later, in December 1991, the Soviet Union collapsed. These events, markers of the end of the Cold War, were seen by many as the final triumphant victory of democracy over authoritarianism and communism. Political scientist Francis Fukuyama famously declared the era to be the "end of history," suggesting that Western-style liberalism was the ultimate form of human ideology. There was a strong consensus—at least in the West—that liberal freedoms were necessary in any society.

But since then, that consensus has been shaken. In the twenty-first century, democracies have crumbled across the globe, with authoritarian leaders grabbing power and eroding traditional rights protections. Examples abound. Mexico and the Philippines embarked on extrajudicial drug wars; Nicolás Maduro's regime brought a state of near-famine to Venezuela; Poland's Law and Justice Party functionally turned parts of the media into its propaganda arm. In countless other countries, leaders have impinged on citizens' freedom. Even the United States—where liberal freedoms have often been taken for granted—has faced powerful movements and leaders who have disputed the legitimacy of the very rights that underpin our democracy.

Yet in the United States, calls to restrict rights have always run up against a powerful adversary, one that dates back to the country's founding: the Constitution of the United States. This Penguin Liberty series is designed to explore the Constitution's protections, illuminating how its text and values can help us as modern citizens to reflect on the meaning of liberty and understand how to defend it. With rights-based democracy under attack from all angles, it is crucial to engage in ongoing discussion about the meaning of liberty, its limits, and its role in the modern world.

Certainly, the ideal of liberty has been present in America since the dawn of the American Revolution, when Patrick Henry reportedly declared, "Give me liberty, or give me death!" In 1776, the Declaration of Independence proclaimed liberty an "unalienable Right"—along with "life" and the "pursuit of Happiness"—enshrining it as a central American aspiration.

These statements, however, are only a start in thinking about liberty. Mistakenly, they seem to suggest that liberty is absolute, never limited. But in this series, we will see that idea continually challenged. Various liberties sometimes conflict, and we must deliberate among them. Importantly, the liberty to be free from government intervention, or what the British philosopher Isaiah Berlin called "negative liberty," must sometimes be balanced against our liberty as a democratic people to govern in the general interest, an idea he called "positive liberty." Thus, the series will also emphasize the importance of liberty not only in terms of freedom from government intervention, but also as self-government, the freedom of all of us collectively to decide on our own destinies.

Ratified in 1788, the Constitution was an attempt to codify the high ideal of liberty as self-government. Through intense debate at the Constitutional Convention, a document was forged that limited government power and gave people a say in how they were to be governed. Its goal was to "secure the Blessings of Liberty to ourselves and our Posterity." Still, many Americans were not convinced the Constitution went far enough in protecting their individual freedom from government coercion—what Berlin would call "negative liberty." Although the push for a Bill of Rights failed at the Constitutional Convention, the First Congress ratified one in 1791. These first ten amendments to the Constitution focused largely on securing individual liberties.

Just over 4,500 words long when originally passed, the U.S. Constitution is the shortest written governing charter of any major democracy. Its brevity belies its impact. Ours is the world's longest surviving written constitution. Some scholars estimate that, at one time, as many as 160 other nations based their constitution at least in part on the U.S. Constitution. The United Nations Universal Declaration of Human Rights from 1948 overlaps significantly with provisions of our Bill of Rights. Individual freedoms that our Constitution champions inspire peoples across the globe.

Of course, the original Constitution protected liberty for only a restricted few. As written in 1787, the Constitution did not explicitly outlaw racialized chattel slavery. Almost 700,000 black people were enslaved in the United States at the time of its founding, a fact that the Constitution did nothing to change and tacitly allowed. Article I prohibited Congress from outlawing the international slave trade until 1808, and the three-fifths clause cemented Southern white political power by having enslaved people count toward political representation without allowing them to vote.

Not all the framers wanted the Constitution to be tainted by slavery. James Madison and Alexander Hamilton, for example, thought slavery morally wrong. But they were willing to compromise this conviction in order for Southern states to ratify the document they so cherished. Thus was born America's original sin, a legally sanctioned system of racial oppression that persisted formally until the Civil War. Only after an estimated more than 600,000 Americans gave their lives in that bloody conflict was the Constitution amended to outlaw slavery, guarantee "equal protection of the laws," and establish that race could deny no citizen access to the franchise.

Enslaved Americans were not the only ones left out of the original Constitution's promise of liberty. Women were guaranteed no formal rights under the Constitution, and they were deprived of equal political status until 1920, when suffragists finally succeeded in amending the Constitution to guarantee women the vote. In the Founding Era, the vote in many states was restricted mainly to white male property owners.

These significant failures are reasons to criticize the Constitution. But they should not lead anyone to discount it altogether. First, the Constitution has demonstrated a remarkable resilience and capacity for change. In each of the cases described above, the Constitution was later amended to attempt to rectify the wrong and expand citizens' rights. Second, and perhaps more important, the Constitution's deepest values have often inspired and strengthened the hand of those seeking justice. That's why Frederick Douglass, himself a former enslaved person, became an ardent supporter of the Constitution, even before the passage of the post–Civil War amendments that ended slavery and provided equal rights. In his Fourth of July oration in 1852, he praised the Constitution as a "glorious liberty document," but added a crucial caveat: it protected liberty only when it was "interpreted as it ought to be interpreted." Douglass believed that while many saw the Constitution as a pro-slavery document, its text and values supported broad protections for freedom and equality.

Douglass's point, though delivered more than 150 years

ago, inspires this Penguin Liberty series. The Constitution is not a static document. Nor is it just a set of provisions on paper. The Constitution is a legal document containing specific rules, but it also gives voice to a broader public morality that transcends any one rule.

What exactly that public morality stands for has always been up for debate and interpretation. Today, after the passage of the post–Civil War amendments, the Constitution takes a clear stand against racial subordination. But there are still many other vital questions of liberty on which the Constitution offers guidance without dictating one definite answer. Through the processes of interpretation, amendment, and debate, the Constitution's guarantees of liberty have, over time, become more fully realized.

In these volumes, we will look to the Constitution's text and values, as well as to American history and some of its most important thinkers, to discover the best explanations of our constitutional ideals of liberty. Though imperfect, the Constitution can be the country's guiding light in dark times, illuminating a path to the recovery of liberty. My hope is that these volumes offer readers the chance to hear the strongest defenses of constitutional ideals, gaining new (or renewed) appreciation for values that have long sustained the nation.

No single fixed or perfectly clear meaning of the Constitution will emerge from this series. Constitutional statements of liberty are often brief, open to multiple interpretations. Competing values within the document raise difficult questions, such as how to balance freedom and equality, or privacy and security. I hope that as you learn from the important texts in these volumes, you undertake a critical examination of what liberty means to you—and how the Constitution should be interpreted to protect it. Though the popular understanding may be that the Supreme Court is the final arbiter of the Constitution, constitutional liberty is best protected when not just every branch of government but also every citizen is engaged in constitutional interpretation. Questions of liberty affect both our daily lives and our country's values, from what we can say to whom we can marry, how society views us to how we determine our leaders. It is Americans' great privilege that we live under a Constitution that both protects our liberty and allows us to debate what that liberty should be.

The central features of constitutional liberty are freedom and equality, values that are often in tension. One of the Constitution's most important declarations of freedom comes in the First Amendment, which provides that "Congress shall make no law respecting an establishment of religion, or prohibiting the free exercise thereof; or abridging the freedom of speech, or of the press; or the right of the people peaceably to assemble, and to petition the Government for a redress of grievances." And one of its most important declarations of equality comes in the Fourteenth Amendment, which reads in part, "no State shall . . . deny to any person within its jurisdiction the equal protection of the laws." These Penguin Liberty volumes look in depth at these conceptions of liberty, while also exploring what mechanisms the Constitution has to protect its guarantees of liberty.

Freedom of speech provides a good place to begin to explore the Constitution's idea of liberty. It is a value that enables both the protection of liberty and the right of citizens to debate its meaning. Textually, the constitutional guarantee that Congress cannot limit free speech might read as though it is absolute. Yet for much of U.S. history, free speech protections were minimal. In 1798, President John Adams

signed the Sedition Act, essentially making it a crime to criticize the president or the U.S. government. During the Civil
War, President Abraham Lincoln had some dissidents and
newspapers silenced. In 1919, a moment came that seemed to
protect free speech, when Justice Oliver Wendell Holmes Jr.
wrote in *Schenck v. United States* that speech could be limited
only when it posed a "clear and present danger." But, in fact,
this ruling did little to protect free speech, as the Court repeatedly interpreted danger so broadly that minority viewpoints,
especially leftist viewpoints, were often seen as imprisonable.

Today, however, U.S. free speech protections are the most
expansive in the world. All viewpoints are allowed to be expressed, except for direct threats and incitements to violence.
Even many forms of hate speech and opinions attacking democracy itself—types of speech that would be illegal in other
countries—are generally permitted here, in the name of free
expression. The Court's governing standard is annunciated in
*Brandenburg v. Ohio*, which protects vast amounts of speech
as long as that speech does not incite "imminent lawless action." How did we get from the Sedition Act to here?

Two thinkers have played an outsize role: John Stuart
Mill and Alexander Meiklejohn. Mill's 1859 classic *On Liberty* is an ode to the idea that both liberty and truth will
thrive in an open exchange of ideas, where all opinions are
allowed to be challenged. In this "marketplace of ideas," as
Mill's idea has often come to be called, the truth stays vibrant
instead of decaying or descending into dogma. Mill's idea explains the virtue of free speech and the importance of a book
series about liberty: Challenging accepted ideas about what
liberty is helps bring the best ideas to light. Meiklejohn's theory focuses more on the connection between free speech and
democracy. To him, the value of free speech is not just for the
speakers, but just as much for the listeners. In a democracy,

only when citizens hear all ideas can they come to informed conclusions about how society should be governed. And only informed citizens can fully exercise other democratic rights besides speech, like the right to vote. Meiklejohn's insistence that democratic citizens need a broad exposure to ideas of liberty inspires this series.

Freedom of religion is another central constitutional value that allows citizens the liberty to be who they are and believe what they wish. It is enshrined in the First Amendment, where the Establishment Clause prevents government endorsement of a religion and the Free Exercise Clause gives citizens the freedom to practice their religion. Though these two religion clauses are widely embraced now, they were radically new at the time of the founding. Among the first European settlers in America were the Puritans, members of a group of English Protestants who were persecuted for their religion in their native Britain. But colonial America did not immediately and totally embrace religious toleration. The Church of England still held great sway in the South during the colonial era, and many states had official religions—even after the Constitution forbade a national religion. At the time the Constitution was ratified, secular government was a rarity.

But religious tolerance was eventually enshrined into the U.S. Constitution, thanks in large part to the influence of two thinkers. British philosopher John Locke opposed systems of theocracy. He saw how government-imposed religious beliefs stifled the freedom of minority believers and imposed religious dogma on unwilling societies. In the United States, James Madison built on Locke's ideas when he drafted the First Amendment. The Free Exercise Clause protected the personal freedom to worship, acknowledging the importance of religious practice among Americans. But on Madison's understanding, the Establishment Clause ensured against theocratic imposition of religion by government. Doing so respected the equality of citizens by refusing to allow the government to favor some people's religious beliefs over others.

A more explicit defense of equality comes from the Equal Protection Clause of the Fourteenth Amendment. But as our volume on the Supreme Court shows, the Constitution has not always been interpreted to promote equality. Before the Civil War, African Americans had few if any formal rights. Millions of African American people were enslaved, and so-called congressional compromises maintained racial subordination long after the importation of slaves was banned in 1808. A burgeoning abolitionist movement gained moral momentum in the North, though the institution of slavery persisted. Liberty was a myth for enslaved people, who were unable to move freely, form organizations, earn wages, or participate in politics.

Still, the Supreme Court, the supposed protector of liberty, for decades failed to guarantee it for African Americans. And in its most notorious ruling it revealed the deep-seated prejudices that had helped to perpetuate slavery. Chief Justice Roger Taney wrote in the 1857 decision in *Dred Scott v. Sandford* that African Americans were not citizens of the United States and "had no rights which the white man was bound to respect." Taney's words were one spark for the Civil War, which, once won by the Union, led to the passage of the Thirteenth, Fourteenth, and Fifteenth Amendments. By ending slavery, granting citizenship and mandating equal legal protection, and outlawing racial discrimination in voting, these Reconstruction Amendments sought to reverse Taney's heinous opinion and provide a platform for advancing real equality.

History unfortunately shows us, however, that legal equality did not translate into real equality for African Americans.

Soon after Reconstruction, the Court eviscerated the Fourteenth Amendment's scope, then ruled in 1896 in *Plessy v. Ferguson* that racial segregation was constitutional if the separate facilities were deemed equal. This paved the way for the legally sanctioned institution of Jim Crow segregation, which relegated African Americans to second-class citizenship, denying them meaningful social, legal, and political equality. Finally, facing immense pressure from civil rights advocates including W. E. B. Du Bois and A. Philip Randolph, as well as the powerful legal reasoning of NAACP lawyer Thurgood Marshall, the Court gave the Equal Protection Clause teeth, culminating in the landmark 1954 *Brown v. Board of Education* decision, which declared that separate is "inherently unequal." Even after that newfound defense of constitutional equality, however, racial inequality has persisted, with the Court and country debating the meaning of liberty and equal protection in issues as varied as affirmative action and racial gerrymandering.

While the Fourteenth Amendment was originally passed with a specific intention to end racial discrimination, its language is general: "No State shall . . . deny to any person within its jurisdiction the equal protection of the laws." Over time, that generality has allowed civil rights advocates to expand the meaning of equality to include other groups facing discrimination. One significant example is the fight for gender equality.

Women had been left out of the Constitution; masculine pronouns pepper the original document, and women are not mentioned. In an 1807 letter to Albert Gallatin, Thomas Jefferson—the person who had penned the Declaration of Independence—wrote that "the appointment of a woman to office is an innovation for which the public is not prepared, nor am I." Liberty was a myth for many women, who were supposed to do little outside the home, had limited rights to property, were often made to be financially dependent on their husbands, and faced immense barriers to political participation.

Nevertheless, women refused to be shut out of politics. Many were influential in the burgeoning temperance and abolition movements of the nineteenth century. In 1848, Elizabeth Cady Stanton wrote the Declaration of Sentiments, amending the Declaration of Independence to include women. Still, suffragists were left out when the Fifteenth Amendment banned voting discrimination based on race— but not on gender. Only after Alice Paul and others led massive protests would the freedom to vote be constitutionally guaranteed for women through the Nineteenth Amendment.

Voting secured one key democratic liberty, but women were still denied the full protection of legal equality. They faced discrimination in the workplace, laws based on sexist stereotypes, and a lack of reproductive autonomy. That's where our volume on Supreme Court justice Ruth Bader Ginsburg begins. Now a feminist icon from her opinions on the Court, Justice Ginsburg earlier served as a litigator with the ACLU, leading their Women's Rights Project, where she helped to convince the Court to consider gender as a protected class under the Fourteenth Amendment. As a justice, she continued her pioneering work to deliver real gender equality, knowing that women would never enjoy the full scope of constitutional liberty unless they held the same legal status as men.

Ginsburg's work underscores how the meaning of constitutional liberty has expanded over time. While the Declaration of Independence did explicitly reference equality, the Bill of Rights did not. Then, with the Reconstruction Amendments, especially the Equal Protection Clause, the Constitution was imbued with a new commitment to equality. Now the document affirmed that democratic societies must protect both negative liberties for citizens to act freely and positive liberties for all to be treated as equal democratic citizens. Never has this tension between freedom and equality been perfectly resolved, but the story of our Constitution is that it has often inspired progress toward realizing liberty for more Americans.

Progress has been possible not just because of an abstract constitutional commitment to liberty, but also due to formal mechanisms that help us to guarantee it. Impeachment is the Constitution's most famous—and most explosive—way to do so. With the abuses of monarchy in mind, the framers needed a way to thwart tyranny and limit concentrated power. Borrowing in language and spirit from the British, who created a system of impeachment to check the power of the king, they wrote this clause into the Constitution: "The President . . . shall be removed from Office on Impeachment for, and Conviction of, Treason, Bribery, or other high Crimes and Misdemeanors."

Early drafts suggested grounds for impeachment should be just "treason or bribery." But George Mason and other delegates objected, wanting impeachable offenses to include broader abuses of power, not just criminal actions. Though Mason's original suggestion of "maladministration" was rejected, the ultimate language of "high Crimes and Misdemeanors" made it possible to pursue impeachment against leaders who threatened the Constitution's deeper values. Impeachment would stand as the ultimate check on officials who have overstepped their constitutional authority.

The House has formally impeached twenty officials throughout American history, and many more have faced some kind of impeachment inquiry. Most of those accused have been federal judges. Just four impeachment proceedings have reached the presidency, the highest echelon of American government. Andrew Johnson, Bill Clinton, and Donald Trump have been formally impeached, though none were removed from office. Richard Nixon resigned after the House Judiciary Committee voted to impeach, before the full House vote could take place. Most of these impeachment proceedings had a background context in which a president was thought to have violated fundamental constitutional liberties—even if that violation was not always the primary component of the impeachment hearings themselves.

For Johnson, although his impeachment focused on the Tenure of Office Act, an underlying issue was his violation of the liberty of newly freed African Americans to live in society as equals. For Nixon, the impeachment inquiry focused on the Watergate break-in and cover-up, which threatened the liberty of voters to have fair elections and a criminally accountable president. For Clinton, who was accused of perjury and obstruction of justice related to a sexual affair with a White House intern, critics argued that his flouting of criminal laws threatened the standard of equal justice under law—a standard necessary for democratic self-government. For Trump, the impeachment articles accused him of soliciting foreign interference as an abuse of power—threatening the liberty of voters to have fair elections. Often, legalistic questions of criminal wrongdoing dominated these impeachment discussions, but concerns about violations of constitutional liberty were always present in the background.

While impeachment is an important remedy for presidential abuse of liberty, liberty lives best when it is respected before crises arise. To do so requires that liberty not be relegated to an idea just for the purview of courts; rather, citizens and officials should engage in discussions about the meaning of liberty, reaffirming its centrality in everyday life.

By few people are those discussions better modeled than by the example of the now hip-hop famous Alexander Hamilton, a founding father and the nation's first secretary of the treasury. Hamilton was a prolific writer, and in our volumes we'll see him square off against other founders in debates on many major challenges facing the early republic. Against Samuel Seabury, Hamilton rejected the British colonial system and said liberty must come through independence. Against Thomas Jefferson (in an argument now immortalized as a Broadway rap battle), Hamilton advocated for a national bank, believing that a modern, industrial economy was needed to grow the nation. Against James Madison, he pushed for stronger foreign policy powers for the president.

The specifics of Hamilton's debates matter. His ideas shaped American notions of government power, from self-determination to economic growth to international engagement. He was instrumental in ratifying the very Constitution that still protects our liberties today. But just as important as *what* he argued for was *how* he argued for it. Hamilton thought deeply about what liberty meant to him, and he engaged in thoughtful, reasoned discussions with people he disagreed with. He cared both for his own freedoms and for the country's welfare at large.

My goal is for readers of these Penguin Liberty volumes to emulate Hamilton's passion for defending his ideas—even, or especially, if they disagree with him on what liberty means. Everyday citizens are the most important readers of this series—and the most important Americans in the struggle to protect and expand constitutional liberty. Without pressure from the citizenry to uphold constitutional ideals, elected leaders can too easily scrap them. Without citizens vigorously examining the meaning of liberty, its power could be lost. Left untended, the flames of liberty could quietly burn out.

The writings in these Penguin Liberty volumes are intended to give citizens the tools to contest and explore the meaning of liberty so it may be kept alive. None of the selections are simple enough to be summed up in tweets or dismissed with quick insults. They are reasoned, thoughtful attempts to defend constitutional ideals of liberty—or warnings about what can happen when those liberties are disregarded. The Constitution's guarantees of liberty have always been aspirations, not realized accomplishments. Yet if these volumes and other constitutional writings inspire us to bring discussions to dinner tables, classrooms, and workplaces across the country, they will be contributing to making those high ideals more real.

COREY BRETTSCHNEIDER

# Introduction

Ruth Bader Ginsburg holds a formal title: Associate Justice of the Supreme Court of the United States. To many fans, though, she is more like a rock star. Multiple popular films and biographies have recently chronicled her life. Her answer to the question of when there will be enough women on the Supreme Court—"When there are nine"—has gone viral. There is even a book chronicling her daily exercise routine. Her popularity is embodied in a nickname: the Notorious RBG.

All this has made Justice Ginsburg a household name. As just the second female Supreme Court justice (Sandra Day O'Connor was the first), it's fitting that she is famous. But Ginsburg's contributions run far deeper than her gender, quips, or push-ups. She has done more than just about any legal mind in American history to demand that constitutional liberty apply equally to women and men. This volume chronicles Justice Ginsburg's efforts to establish gender equality, working to change both the law and the thinking of her fellow Americans. To Ginsburg, only when women and men stand on an equal playing field in society can the Constitution protect the liberty of all.

Ginsburg's journey began far from the position of power

she occupies today. Born as Joan Ruth Bader in 1933, she grew up in a working-class neighborhood in Brooklyn, New York. Her mother battled cancer during Ginsburg's high school years, and died before she graduated. After graduating from college, Ginsburg worked for the Social Security Administration, where she was essentially demoted after becoming pregnant with her daughter. Angered but not defeated by that discrimination, she made it to Harvard Law School, which she attended alongside her husband, Martin Ginsburg. While there, Martin was diagnosed with cancer, leaving Ginsburg to help him complete his assignments while he was in treatment and recovery, all while also attending her own classes, completing her own coursework, and raising their child. Ruth ultimately transferred to Columbia Law School and graduated first in her class.

A male colleague with her résumé would have had no trouble finding work. But Ginsburg saw rejection letters pile up. She secured a clerkship only after her constitutional law professor Gerald Gunther demanded that a federal judge hire her, lest Gunther never recommend another Columbia student to him. From there Ginsburg went on to a teaching job at Rutgers Law School, though discrimination followed her as one of fewer than twenty female law professors in the country; she was paid less than her male counterparts, and joined an equal pay campaign at the school in protest.

These experiences with injustice animated the next steps in Ginsburg's career. In 1970, she became the founding faculty advisor of the *Women's Rights Law Reporter* at Rutgers, the nation's first law review devoted exclusively to gender issues. She also took her fight directly to the courtroom, and in 1972 cofounded the new Women's Rights Project at the ACLU, designed to challenge laws that discriminated against women.

But before we read her pathbreaking efforts, it's worth noting the context that demanded Ginsburg take up the cause. In 1972, almost two hundred years after the Constitution was ratified, gender discrimination in the law was common and often not seen as unconstitutional.

The text of the original Constitution makes no mention of women. All the pronouns are masculine. Even the Declaration of Independence proclaims "all *men* are created equal" (emphasis added). Not shockingly, based on those facts, no women were delegates to the Constitutional Convention, and the few women who did try to influence politics were outliers. During the Founding Era, women were often seen as subservient to men, were not allowed to vote, had limited rights to property, and were denied many forms of education. The list of inequalities could go on.

Still, Ginsburg's genius was being able to use a part of the Constitution that did not explicitly protect gender equality— the Fourteenth Amendment—to advance the cause. The Fourteenth Amendment reads: "No State shall . . . deny to any person within its jurisdiction the equal protection of the laws." Note the language of "person," not "man." No one can deny that the Fourteenth Amendment, passed after the Civil War, was designed specifically to thwart racial discrimination. However, its framers did leave the amendment open-ended enough that a brilliant scholar such as Ginsburg could have just enough room to work.

Before Ginsburg was able to take on her work expanding the application of the Equal Protection Clause, a suffrage movement had demanded and gained a more basic democratic liberty: the right to vote. In many localities well into the 1800s, only white, propertied, adult men were able to vote. After the Civil War, the Republican Party and African Americans finally won their fight to expand the franchise, culminating in the Fifteenth Amendment: "The right of citizens . . . to vote shall not be denied or abridged . . . on account of race, color, or previous condition of servitude." It was the most affirmative statement of voting rights found in the Constitution at the time.

Women were conspicuously left out. That was a purposeful, though difficult, choice. Partly determining that African Americans were more at risk, Reconstruction Republicans left gender out of the Fifteenth Amendment's voting rights protections. It would take an entirely new suffrage movement, pushed by provocative leaders such as Alice Paul, to finally write voting equality for women into the Constitution via the Nineteenth Amendment, ratified on August 18, 1920: "The right of citizens . . . to vote shall not be denied or abridged . . . on account of sex."

The Fifteenth Amendment's omission now rectified, Ginsburg took up the cause a half century later of making the Fourteenth Amendment more inclusive of women. She had allies in the political branches, with female members of Congress helping to ensure that protections for discrimination based on sex were written into the 1964 Civil Rights Act. Furthermore, as Ginsburg was building her litigation strategy, a separate movement was pushing for the ratification of the Equal Rights Amendment, declaring that "[e]quality of rights under the law shall not be denied or abridged . . . on account of sex."

Ginsburg supported the passage of the ERA. But her contributions have come more as a scholar and lawyer than as an activist protesting on the front lines. In this volume we will see how Ginsburg has used a painstaking approach to constitutional interpretation to try to realize the promise of legal gender equality in America. Her legal efforts undergird broader societal goals: for women to have equal status with men, to be offered the same opportunities to realize their potential, to be free from the burdens of regressive laws or outdated stereotypes. As they are achieved, these goals help to secure for women the positive liberty of self-government that the Constitution once guaranteed only for propertied white men.

Ginsburg's fight for legal gender equality has been multifaceted. She began by publishing scholarly articles on gender equality that countered common notions in the legal field. Then she took to the courts, using her litigation position with the ACLU to advocate for her views on women's rights. Finally, she was appointed to the federal bench and then to the Supreme Court, where she has incorporated her inclusive views of gender equality into her constitutional interpretation and rulings.

Ginsburg has not always been on the winning side of her fights. She has become famous for her biting dissents. (Her dissent in *Burwell v. Hobby Lobby Stores, Inc.*, for example, featured in this volume, was the basis for a viral song.) But we should appreciate these dissents for more than just their meme-worthy lines. Having the courage to dissent from prevailing views allowed Ginsburg to fight for the idea that the Fourteenth Amendment's true values must include women— a position that was not uniformly accepted in the 1970s, when she started with the ACLU. And now that this view has become commonplace, Ginsburg continues to push forward; her dissents from the bench often sketch a vision of a future with equal rights for all.

Ginsburg's dissents should remind us of a crucial component of liberty, one explored further in the Penguin Liberty volume on free speech: that the right to dissent is essential to freedom. Only when all views are heard can citizens make informed decisions, and only when minority voices are empowered can we find the best ideas.

Over the course of her career, Ginsburg's most important writings on liberty have focused around three themes: equal protection for women, reproductive freedom, and civil rights. Each fits into her overall vision of liberty: that the Constitution requires all persons to have equal status and standing in society, without discrimination against women and racial minorities.

Ginsburg has advanced gender equality most directly through the Equal Protection Clause. At the ACLU, she faced the tall order of convincing courts and society that gender-based discrimination was unconstitutional. She wanted to appeal not just to legal principles but also to the common-sense idea that people should not be treated differently for no good reason. If she could show that the Constitution prohibited clearly irrational discrimination against women, she would lay the groundwork for ruling that less blatant (but still harmful) forms of discrimination were also illegal. All she needed was a litigant who had been as blatantly discriminated against as she had been in her search for a clerkship or in her equal pay battle at Rutgers.

She found one in a 1970 case called *Reed v. Reed*. When Sally Reed's son died, her estranged husband was appointed administrator of the estate because Idaho's law preferred men to women for the role. Sally Reed thought the role belonged to her. To make Sally Reed's case, Ginsburg drew on the Equal Protection Clause to push a two-part argument we'll see throughout this section: Laws that classify women differently from men should be inherently suspect; laws that unfairly discriminate against women or make them second-class citizens are unconstitutional when they unfairly discriminate against women and make them second-class citizens. The

Supreme Court partially agreed, ruling Idaho's law drew an arbitrary and unconstitutional distinction between men and women.

Count that as a victory for Ginsburg. Still, her goal was to make gender discrimination unconstitutional even when it was not blatantly arbitrary. To do so, she weighed in on the *Craig v. Boren* case by submitting an amicus curiae—or "friend of the court"—brief. This case dealt with an Oklahoma law that allowed women age eighteen to buy beer with less than 3.2 percent alcohol, while men had to wait until they were twenty-one to do so. Some might see that as a win for women. After all, for once, they're the beneficiary of the unequal treatment!

Ginsburg saw through that rationale. She recognized that the law was stereotyping young women as more mature than young men. And no matter how positive the stereotype, laws that treat men and women differently "shore up artificial barriers to full realization by men and women of their human potential, and . . . retard progress toward equal opportunity, free from gender-based discrimination." In other words, constitutional liberty requires not just freedom to act but also freedom from the burden of society's gendered expectations.

In *Craig v. Boren*, the Court, while not adopting Ginsburg's full view, took her side in the case, striking down Oklahoma's law. The opinion noted that Oklahoma's generalizations about drinking patterns were "invidious discrimination." The Court also wrote that future gender discrimination cases like these, in which there is an explicit distinction in the law based on sex, should be reviewed under a standard now known to lawyers as "intermediate scrutiny." This standard demands that any law explicitly distinguishing people based on sex needs to be justified by an "important" governmental interest and be "substantially related" to that interest, a step closer to Ginsburg's ideal of classifying gender as a suspect classification.

Ginsburg had even more opportunity to shape the law when she joined the Supreme Court. One of her biggest contributions came in *United States v. Virginia*. The Virginia Military Institute was an elite leadership school that excluded women on grounds that its "adversarial method" of education would be undermined absent a single-sex male environment. Ginsburg and the majority of her colleagues recognized that VMI's rationale for its single-sex model was founded on stereotypes that unfairly and unnecessarily disadvantaged women. In a historic 7–1 ruling, the Court solidified the elevated standard of constitutional protection the Fourteenth Amendment offers women. The Constitution protects against not just irrational discrimination but also discrimination that lacks an "important" purpose that was "substantially related" to the law at hand. Her "skeptical scrutiny" standard—or, as it's commonly called, intermediate scrutiny—made clear that women could not be discriminated against simply because of their sex.

Ginsburg's vision of gender equality has not always been the prevailing view on the Court. One loss that particularly stung came in a pay equity case called *Ledbetter v. Goodyear Tire and Rubber Co., Inc.* Women had been included in the 1964 Civil Rights Act, a sign of broader societal awareness of gender discrimination. That was not broad enough to protect Lilly Ledbetter, a manager at the Goodyear Tire Company who had been paid less than her male counterparts for decades, with the gap growing over time. The Court ruled against her essentially on a technicality, saying that she missed the deadline to file her pay gap complaint. The majority interpreted the Civil Rights Act to start the clock for the statute of limitations only the first time an employee receives less pay for equal work. None of the subsequent discrimination against Ms. Ledbetter, paycheck after paycheck, year after year, would extend the deadline any further. Justice Ginsburg rejected this narrow and formalistic reading of such landmark legislation that was intended to prohibit employment discrimination "because of sex." Her biting dissent charged that "the Court does not comprehend, or is indifferent to, the insidious way in which women can be victims of pay discrimination."

Ginsburg lost the fight but won the war. In 2009, Congress passed the Lilly Ledbetter Fair Pay Act, extending the filing deadline for victims of discrimination every time they are discriminated against. Ginsburg had found a creative way to change the law. Her dissent played no small part in inspiring this legislation, keeping open the courthouse doors for people like Lilly Ledbetter, who was denied the pay she deserved simply because she was a woman.

Our second section deals with reproductive freedom, a cause Ginsburg sees as closely bound with gender equality. In 1973, *Roe v. Wade* established a constitutional right to have an abortion, and *Roe* is still central in today's abortion debates. Ginsburg might have preferred it if the Court had charted a different path.

She supports the right of women to terminate a pregnancy. She just believes that *Roe* did not adequately discuss a fundamental justification for abortion rights. *Roe* focused on the right to privacy, which Ginsburg finds important. To her, however, just as important, if not more so, is the right of women to have equal standing in society with men—a right she believed was protected by the Fourteenth Amendment's Equal Protection Clause. When women are subjected to disadvantageous treatment—in health care, employment, or other fields—simply because they are pregnant, they are being treated unequally. When women are forced to bear the burden of childbirth and child-rearing, they are less able than men to freely chart the course of their own lives.

One case that could have put the Equal Protection Clause front and center in the abortion jurisprudence was *Struck v. Secretary of Defense*. Captain Susan Struck had been ordered to be honorably discharged from the Air Force after she became pregnant, per existing Air Force policy. To Ginsburg, as she later put it in her Supreme Court confirmation hearing, "if you subject a woman to disadvantageous treatment on the basis of her pregnant status, which was what was happening to Captain Struck, you would be denying her equal treatment under the law." The focus on privacy in *Roe* was important. It just wouldn't give women as much protection as an affirmation that no law can punish them for their decision to have or not have a child—a decision only women have to make. Pretending that discrimination against pregnant people is not gender discrimination masks gender bias in the law.

Here Ginsburg has not been as often on the winning side of the issue. *Roe* is still the hallmark abortion case, in part because *Struck* was settled privately before it reached the Supreme Court. Later cases of *Geduldig v. Aiello* and *General Electric Company v. Gilbert* ruled that pregnancy distinctions in the denial of health or disability benefits are not always gender discrimination.

That put her in an odd spot while serving on the Court. Perhaps feeling bound by precedent, as a justice she has followed *Roe* and has largely avoided invoking her view of abortion rights developed in *Struck*. Through this role Ginsburg's pragmatism has shined, as she has creatively searched for ways to ensure that women are not subjected to worse treatment either for being pregnant or for choosing to have an abortion. That pragmatic focus was illustrated, for instance, in her concurrence in *Whole Woman's Health v. Hellerstedt*, in which she emphasized the dangers of reversing abortion rights protections. She wrote there, "[w]hen a State severely limits access to safe and legal procedures, women in desperate circumstances may resort to unlicensed rogue practitioners . . . at great risk to their health and safety."

In *Gonzales v. Carhart*, Ginsburg dissented from the majority's willingness to limit the abortion right. To Ginsburg, the Court's upholding of a "partial-birth abortion" ban violated women's reproductive autonomy. Her dissent spilled much ink on the majority's factually wrong understanding of the associated medical procedures. Yet she still managed to tie the privacy question to one of equality: "legal challenges to undue restrictions on abortion procedures . . . center on a woman's autonomy to determine her life's course, and thus to enjoy equal citizenship stature."

Ginsburg's framing of reproductive rights as a matter of equal citizenship has remained in the minority on the Court. In *Burwell v. Hobby Lobby Stores, Inc.*, Ginsburg dissented from an opinion that allowed employers to opt out of contraceptive coverage for religious reasons. She grounded her arguments about statutory interpretation of the Religious Freedom Restoration Act in an insight about constitutional values and the connection between liberty and gender equality. Quoting Justice Sandra Day O'Connor's opinion in the major abortion case of *Planned Parenthood of Southeastern Pennsylvania v. Casey*, she emphasized that "[t]he ability of women to participate equally in the economic and social life of the Nation has been facilitated by their ability to control their reproductive lives."

Our third section explores Ginsburg's expansive view of the Equal Protection Clause as a tool to secure all citizens—

regardless of race, gender, sexual orientation, or other marginalized identity—equal status under law. A critic might
accuse Ginsburg in the "near beer" case, *Craig v. Boren*, of
focusing too much on the distinctions between men and
women, rather than on the societal subjection of women to
men. But that would get her jurisprudence wrong. For Ginsburg, what was wrong with the "near beer" law was that stereotypes about women do hurt them, perpetuating false ideas
and treating them as less able to determine the course of their
own lives. She believed stereotypes about women that in-
fringed on their freedom or treated them as less than men
could not stand scrutiny.

That broad focus on subordination has animated Ginsburg's work in discrimination cases dealing with issues beyond gender, especially issues around race. However, the
robust protections for equality that Ginsburg supports have
often been relegated to dissents. Race-based distinctions, to
her, often subordinate people of color and minority groups,
just like gender-based distinctions do to women. Ginsburg's
view of liberty does not involve being race- or gender-blind,
but rather taking active steps to ensure that classifications,
stereotypes, or outright discrimination do not prevent
marginalized groups from full participation in society.

This volume concludes with four dissents and one majority opinion in cases dealing with civil rights. In *Adarand
Constructors, Inc. v. Peña* and *Ricci v. DeStefano*, Ginsburg's
dissents defend the use of race in affirmative action as the way
we ensure that the Equal Protection Clause and the Civil
Rights Act actually deliver equality to the people they were
written to protect. Her dissent in *Shelby County v. Holder*
continues her focus on racial discrimination, as she decries
the Court's decision striking down part of the 1965 Voting
Rights Act that aimed to protect African American voters'

access to the franchise as a fundamental threat to the promise of democracy. Showing the depth of her commitment to the marginalized, her majority opinion in *Olmstead v. L.C.* is a powerful endorsement of the idea that a disability should not prevent anyone from full participation in public life. Whereas most of these dissents decry an unwillingness to use the Equal Protection Clause, Ginsburg's dissent in *Bush v. Gore* criticizes a misplaced attempt to use the clause to override a decision by the Florida Supreme Court.

Few people have done more than Ginsburg to embed liberty more deeply into the law. She stands with Thurgood Marshall, the lawyer who masterminded the legal strategy that helped lead to the end of legalized racial segregation, on the Mount Rushmore of America's great legal minds. Ginsburg's work has shined a light that cannot be put out on the ways the law has subjugated and continues to subjugate women. In victory and dissent, she has put forward a vision of a Constitution that protects women and all other citizens on a truly equal basis. The pages that follow are a testament to her—the popular icon, yes, but also the brilliant legal mind whose influence has played a critical role in the project of constitutional liberty.

COREY BRETTSCHNEIDER

# A Note on the Text

All of the following writings of Justice Ginsburg are selected excerpts from her work as a lawyer and jurist. All citations have been removed, without notation. Spelling and punctuation are in the original. Readers can find full text citations for sources in the Unabridged Source Materials section. Not all excerpts begin with the original text's opening phrases.

The legal briefs included here were submitted to the Supreme Court by Ginsburg, writing with other attorneys, while working as a law professor and as a lawyer with the American Civil Liberties Union. Quotes to begin each section are from the transcript of Justice Ginsburg's Supreme Court confirmation hearing in the Senate. Supreme Court opinions of which Justice Ginsburg is the author are listed as "Majority Opinion." Writings from cases in which Justice Ginsburg voted against the Court's majority opinion are listed as "Dissenting Opinion." Writings from cases in which Ginsburg concurred with the majority decision in the case but wanted to emphasize a distinct reasoning for her vote are listed as "Concurring Opinion."

*Decisions and Dissents of*

# JUSTICE
# RUTH BADER
# GINSBURG

# Part I

# GENDER EQUALITY
## and
# WOMEN'S RIGHTS

Indeed, in my lifetime, I expect to see three, four, perhaps even more women on the high court bench, women not shaped from the same mold, but of different complexions. Yes, there are miles in front; but what a distance we have traveled from the day President Thomas Jefferson told his secretary of state, "The appointment of women to public office is an innovation for which the public is not prepared." "Nor," Jefferson added, "am I."

—RUTH BADER GINSBURG,
SENATE CONFIRMATION HEARING, JULY 20, 1993

## Brief for the Appellant in *Reed v. Reed* (1971)

*In 1971, while a professor at Rutgers Law School and not yet a judge, Ruth Bader Ginsburg cowrote with ACLU lawyers a brief for the appellant in a case called Reed v. Reed, decided in 1971. Sally Reed's son had recently died, and she and her separated husband, Cecil, were engaged in a battle over who would administer their son's estate. In Idaho, where the Reeds lived, state law dictated that Cecil was entitled to be the administrator, because "males must be preferred to females." Ginsburg was interested in the case not just to assert Sally Reed's right to be an administrator but to make a broader point about how laws that arbitrarily privilege men over women violate the Fourteenth Amendment's Equal Protection Clause. In the brief, Ginsburg argues forcefully that the Idaho law is unconstitutional.*

. . . The issue in this case is whether, as appellant contends, mandatory disqualification of a woman for appointment as an administrator, whenever a man "equally entitled to administer" applies for appointment, constitutes arbitrary and unequal treatment proscribed by the fourteenth amendment to the United States Constitution. . . .

In very recent years, a new appreciation of women's place has been generated in the United States. Activated by feminists of both sexes, courts and legislatures have begun to recognize the claim of women to full membership in the class "persons" entitled to due process guarantees of life and liberty and the equal protection of the laws. But the distance to equal opportunity for women—in the face of the pervasive social, cultural and legal roots of sex-based discrimination—remains considerable. In the absence of a firm constitutional foundation for equal treatment of men and women by the law, women seeking to be judged on their individual merits will continue to encounter law-sanctioned obstacles. . . .

The experience of trying to root out racial discrimination in the United States has demonstrated that even when the arsenal of legislative and judicial remedies is well stocked, social and cultural institutions shaped by centuries of law-sanctioned bias do not crumble under the weight of legal pronouncements proscribing discrimination. Thus . . . sex-based discrimination will not disintegrate upon this Court's recognition that sex is a suspect classification. But without this recognition, the struggle for an end to sex-based discrimination will extend well beyond the current period in time, a period in which any functional justification for difference in treatment has ceased to exist.

*One challenge Ginsburg faced in writing the brief was that the Supreme Court had never used the Equal Protection Clause to strike down a law because it discriminated on the basis of sex. Sex discrimination had not been the focus of the Fourteenth Amendment's framers. Ginsburg needed to show that sex discrimination*

*was at least partially analagous to race discrimination: both were*
*arbitrary forms of unequal treatment. At the time, this view was*
*contested; many people thought that men and women were simply*
*biologically different, and the law should reflect that. In the next*
*section, Ginsburg begins the monumental task of arguing that sex*
*should be a "suspect classification," not an acceptable reason to treat*
*people differently under law.*

It is only within the last half-dozen years that the light of
constitutional inquiry has focused upon sex discrimination.
Emerging from this fresh examination, in the context of the
significant changes that have occurred in society's attitudes,
is a deeper appreciation of the premise underlying the "suspect classification" doctrine: although the legislature may
distinguish between individuals on the basis of their ability
or need, it is presumptively impermissible to distinguish on
the basis of congenital and unalterable biological traits of
birth over which the individual has no control and for which
he or she should not be penalized. Such conditions include
not only race, a matter clearly within the "suspect classification" doctrine, but include as well the sex of the individual. . . .

. . . Through a process of social evolution, racial distinctions have become unacceptable. The old social consensus
that race was a clear indication of inferiority has yielded to the
notion that race is unrelated to ability or performance. Even
allegedly rational attempts at racial classification are now
generally rejected outright. The burden of showing that these
attempts are based on something other than prejudice is
enormous.

There are indications that sex classifications may be un-
dergoing a similar metamorphosis in the public mind. Once
thought normal, proper, and ordained in the "very nature of

things," sex discrimination may soon be seen as a sham, not unlike that perpetrated in the name of racial superiority. Whatever differences may exist between the sexes, legislative judgments have frequently been based on inaccurate stereotypes of the capacities and sensibilities of women. In view of the damage that has been inflicted on individuals in the name of these "differences," any continuing distinctions should, like race, bear a heavy burden of proof. One function of the fourteenth amendment ought to be to put such broad-ranging concerns into the fundamental law of the land. . . .

When biological differences are not related to the activity in question, sex-based discrimination clashes with contemporary notions of fair and equal treatment. No longer shackled by decisions reflecting social and economic conditions or legal and political theories of an earlier era, both federal and state courts have been intensely skeptical of lines drawn or sanctioned by governmental authority on the basis of sex. Absent strong affirmative justification, these lines have not survived constitutional scrutiny. . . .

Another characteristic which underlies all suspect classifications is the stigma of inferiority and second class citizenship associated with them. Women, like Negroes, aliens, and the poor have historically labored under severe legal and social disabilities. Like black citizens, they were, for many years, denied the right to vote and, until recently, the right to serve on juries in many states. They are excluded from or discriminated against in employment and educational opportunities. Married women in particular have been treated as inferior persons in numerous laws relating to property and independent business ownership and the right to make contracts.

Laws which disable women from full participation in the political, business and economic arenas are often characterized as "protective" and beneficial. Those same laws applied to racial or ethnic minorities would readily be recognized as invidious and impermissible. The pedestal upon which women have been placed has all too often, upon closer inspection, been revealed as a cage. We conclude that the sexual classifications are properly treated as suspect, particularly when those classifications are made with respect to a fundamental interest such as employment.

*To prove that sex should be a suspect classification, Ginsburg needed to make a second point, beyond just that biology cannot justify unequal treatment. She also needed to prove that women faced real discrimination—just like African Americans, discrimination against whom was the original basis for the Equal Protection Clause. In the next section, Ginsburg does so by attacking the typical justifications given for sex-classified laws.*

While the characteristics that make a classification "suspect" have not been defined explicitly by this Court . . . a series of cases delineates as the principal factor the presence of an unalterable identifying trait which the dominant culture views as a badge of inferiority justifying disadvantaged treatment in social, legal, economic and political contexts. Although the paradigm suspect classification is, of course, one based on race, this Court has made it plain that the doctrine is not confined to a "two-class theory." . . .

American women have been stigmatized historically as an inferior class and are today subject to pervasive discrimination. As other groups that have been assisted toward full equality via the suspect classification doctrine, women lack political power to remedy the discriminatory treatment they are accorded in the law and in society generally. . . .

No doubt promotion of expeditious administration of estates and curtailment of litigation are bona fide state interests. But it is equally plain that the end of expediency cannot be served by unconstitutional means. . . .

The fact that not all women are denied the right to a hearing or presumed less than competent to administer an estate highlights the invidious discrimination inherent in the statute. A woman may compete on terms of equality whenever her challenger is another woman. If no male equally eligible opposes, the woman will be appointed. Through this device of law-mandated subordination of "equally entitled" women to men, the dominant male society, exercising its political power, has secured women's place as the second sex. . . .

*Ginsburg's ideal outcome in this case was for the Court to make gender a "suspect classification," establishing the basis for striking down other laws treating women with less dignity than men. Her role with the ACLU, however, required her to be more than just an idealist; she had to win the case she was litigating. That meant her back-up plan was to push the Court to make a narrower claim: that irrational instances of treating women worse than men were violations of the Equal Protection Clause—even if not every instance of gender discrimination was suspect.*

. . . Attributable in part to decisions of this Court, women continue to receive disadvantaged treatment by the law. In answer to the compelling claim of women for recognition by the law as full human personalities, this Court, at the very least, should reverse the presumption of a statute's rationality when the statute accords a preference to males. Rather than require the party attacking the statute to show that the classification is irrational, the Court should require the statute's proponent to prove it rational. . . .

Declaring that "nature itself has established the distinction," the Idaho Supreme Court seemingly justified the discrimination challenged here by finding it "rational" to assume the mental inferiority of women to men. This assumption, particularized in the judgment that "men are better qualified to act as an administrator than are women" demands swift condemnation of this Court. . . .

Any legislative judgment that "men are better qualified to act as an administrator than are women" is simply untenable. . . . Moreover, although the Idaho Supreme Court did not provide any enlightenment on the specific functions an administrator performs for which "men are better qualified," the standard responsibilities are evident: receiving payments from creditors, paying out debts, paying state and federal taxes if any, preserving the assets of the estate, and finally paying out the net estate to the lawful heirs. Except for the occasional millionaire who dies intestate, the responsibilities are hardly onerous. They can be handled satisfactorily by most people who have completed secondary school education. . . .

Finally, as developed in the preceding section, Idaho's interest in prompt administration of estates and curtailment of litigation is barely served by section 15-314. The male preference system operates in relatively few cases. In most situations in which more than one applicant from a class of equal eligibles separately seek letters of administration, hearings must be held. Indeed, and quite appropriately, the Idaho Code invites hearings by providing that "any person interested" may challenge the competency of the administrator.

To eliminate women who share an eligibility category with a man, when there is no basis in fact to assume that women are less competent to administer than are men, is patently unreasonable and constitutionally impermissible. A woman's right to equal treatment may not be sacrificed to expediency.

*Ultimately, it was Ginsburg's narrower claim that won. The Supreme Court ruled unanimously in* Reed v. Reed *that Idaho's law favoring men over women was "the very kind of arbitrary legislative choice forbidden by the Equal Protection Clause of the Fourteenth Amendment." Though neglecting to say that all gender-based distinctions were arbitrary, the Court still ruled in a way that allowed for Ginsburg to make future arguments defending a more robust role for gender protections under the Fourteenth Amendment.*

# Brief of the American Civil Liberties Union, *Amicus Curiae*, in *Craig v. Boren* (1976)

*Ruth Bader Ginsburg is known as a champion of women's rights. Sometimes to expand those rights, however, she had to take an unusual path. In the following brief, Ginsburg's unusual path involves defending a law that seemed to advantage women. In 1976, Ginsburg, then director of the Women's Rights Project at the ACLU, cowrote an amicus curiae brief in the case of* Craig v. Boren. *In this "friend of the court" brief—a legal document submitted to the Court by a group or individual not directly involved in the litigation—Ginsburg argues against an Oklahoma law that allowed women to purchase low-alcohol beer at an earlier age than men. Careless critics might think Ginsburg's position in the brief suggested that discrimination against men was as serious or prevalent as discrimination against women. A closer look at her brief, however, shows her view to be far more nuanced, her goals still laser-focused on real equality for women—and thus equality for all. To Ginsburg, demanding that the Court give close scrutiny to any law that drew distinctions based on gender would bolster her victory in* Reed v. Reed *and call attention to the ways that legal stereotypes can hurt women, even when they appear beneficial. Ginsburg's outline of her argument follows.*

# SUMMARY OF ARGUMENT

## I

. . . Establishing a sex/age line to determine qualification for association with 3.2 beer, discriminates impermissibly on the basis of gender in violation of the fourteenth amendment's equal protection clause. This legislation places all 18–20 year old males in one pigeonhole, all 18–20 year old females in another, in conformity with familiar notions about "the way women (or men) are." Upholding the legislation, the court below relied upon overbroad generalizations concerning the drinking behavior, proclivities and preferences of the two sexes. Such overbroad generalization as a rationalization for line-drawing by gender cannot be tolerated under the Constitution. . . .

On the surface, Oklahoma's 3.2 beer sex/age differential may appear to accord young women a liberty withheld from young men. Upon deeper inspection, the gender line drawn by Oklahoma is revealed as a manifestation of traditional attitudes about the expected behavior of males and females, part of the myriad signals and messages that daily underscore the notion of men as society's active members, women as men's quiescent companions.

## II

. . . Just as drinking preferences and proclivities associated with a particular ethnic group or social class would be perceived as an unfair and insubstantial basis for a beverage sale or service prohibition directed to that group or class, so a gender-based classification should be recognized as an inappropriate, invidious means to the legislative end of rational regulation in the public interest. . . .

## III

. . . The legislation in question is a bizarre and paradoxical remnant of the day when "anything goes" was the rule for line-drawing by gender.

*Her argument laid out, Ginsburg goes on to dive deeper into the ways that gender-based distinctions are at odds with the Court's precedents. After* Reed v. Reed, *the Court had become more insistent that mere stereotypes or assumptions about women did not provide a sufficiently rational or compelling basis for a law. In the following section, Ginsburg shows the Court how even in this case, when the stereotype seems to be about men, the Court must be consistent in its application of the law if gender distinctions are in play.*

## I

### A

Since *Reed v. Reed*, 404 U.S. 71 (1971), this Court has instructed consistently that gender-based legislative classification, premised on overbroad generalization concerning the behavior, proclivities and preferences of the two sexes, cannot be tolerated under the Constitution. The decision below rests exclusively upon such overbroad generalization. That decision, and the gender line it upholds, merit this Court's decisive disapprobation. . . .

. . . In short, the essence of this Court's decisions con-
demning laws drawing "a sharp line between the sexes" es-
caped appellees and the court below: neither unsubstantiated
stereotypes nor generalized factual data suffice to justify pi-
geonholing by gender; a legislature may not place all males
in one pigeonhole, all females in another, based on assumed
or documented notions about "the way women or men are."

The sole post-*Reed* cases in which this Court has counte-
nanced classification based on "gender as such" involved legislation justified as compensating women for past and present
economic disadvantage. But Oklahoma's action cannot be rationalized on the ground that nowadays, females may be favored, but not disfavored by the law. For surely the concept
"compensatory" or "rectificatory" gender classification does
not encompass the solace 3.2 beer might provide to young
women already exposed to society's double standards or
about to encounter an inhospitable job market. . . .

*Ginsburg was not content with just winning a case about "near
beer." She was determined to shape the law going forward, em-
phasizing that gender stereotyping hurts women, even when it
seemingly protects them. In the next passage, she argues that the
Constitution disallows distinctions based on sexist assumptions
that put women on a pedestal while restricting their opportunities.*

This case involves more than an impermissible sex/age differential. It also involves the lore relating to women and liquor—
a combination that has fascinated lawmen for generations.
The legislation at issue is a manifestation, with a bizarre
twist, of the erstwhile propensity of legislatures to prescribe
the conditions under which women and alcohol may mix. In

recent years, however, outside Oklahoma, such legislation has been relegated to history's scrap heap. As the Court of Appeals for the First Circuit said of once traditional judicial essays in this area, "the authority of those precedents . . . has waned with the metamorphosis of the attitudes which fed them. What was then gallantry now appears Victorian condescension or even misogyny, and this cultural evolution is now reflected in the Constitution." . . .

It bears emphasis that no legislative history informed the conjecture of the court below as to the lawmaker's design. Post hoc attempts to hypothesize an appropriate rationale, though once routinely accepted where gender lines were at issue, are no longer immune from close scrutiny. Moreover, no legislative design has been advanced that would even remotely satisfy the constitutional requirement that, at the least, gender-based classification must be "reasonable, not arbitrary, and must rest upon some ground of difference having a fair and substantial relation to the object of the legislation. . . ." For gender is no more rational or less arbitrary a criterion upon which to base liquor or traffic safety laws than is religion or national origin. . . . [The] three-judge court's readiness to accept the gender line as unobjectionable warrant prompt correction by this Court.

## D

Oklahoma's sex/age 3.2 beer line may appear at first glance a sport, a ridiculous distinction. In comparison to other business vying for this Court's attention, [it] might be viewed as supplying comic relief. Yet if this Oklahoma legislative action is not checked, if the overbroad generalizations tendered in its support are allowed to stand as proof adequate to justify a gender-based criterion, then this Court will have turned back the clock to the day when "anything goes" was the approach to line drawing by gender. For any defender of a gender line, with a modicum of sophistication, could avoid express reliance on "old notions" and, instead, invoke statistics to "demonstrate the facts of life." But this Court's recent precedent should stand as a bulwark against "the imposition of special disabilities upon the members of a particular sex because of their sex." . . .

On its face, Oklahoma's 3.2 beer differential accords young women a liberty withheld from young men. Upon deeper inspection, however, the discrimination is revealed as simply another manifestation of traditional attitudes and prejudices about the expected behavior and roles of the two sexes in our society, part of the myriad signals and messages that daily underscore the notion of men as society's active members, women as men's quiescent companions, members of the "other" or second sex.

Laws such as [Oklahoma's] serve only to shore up artificial barriers to full realization by men and women of their human potential, and to retard progress toward equal opportunity, free from gender-based discrimination. Ultimately harmful to women by casting the weight of the state on the side of traditional notions concerning woman's behavior and her relation to man, such laws have no place in a nation preparing to celebrate a 200-year commitment to equal justice under law.

*Ginsburg's argument again won the day. Seven to two, the Court ruled that the Oklahoma law was based on faulty statistics and relied impermissibly on gender stereotypes. Significantly, the decision showed the Court moving closer to adopting Ginsburg's view that gender-based distinctions should be reviewed with suspicion.*

*Instead of evaluating gender distinctions under the lowest "rational basis" standard, the Court would use a new standard—commonly known as intermediate scrutiny—to ensure that laws drawing distinctions between men and women were justified appropriately. Though not applying the highest "strict scrutiny" standard Ginsburg had at times argued for, the Court took a major step toward considering sex a "suspect classification," as Ginsburg had demanded in* Reed.

# Majority Opinion in
# *United States v. Virginia* (1996)

*Justice Ginsburg began her litigation career by seeking
out examples of sex discrimination so egregious that the
Court would have to say that the Equal Protection
Clause applies to women. Those early cases she won as
a litigator would become building blocks for the more
expansive protection she has helped women secure as a
Supreme Court justice.* United States v. Virginia *was
one of her crowning achievements in this area. The
commonwealth of Virginia operated the Virginia Military Institute, an all-male leadership school. The United
States government sued to open its doors to women.
Writing for the majority, Ginsburg, now a Supreme
Court justice, here solidifies some of the ideas she had
advocated as a litigator: gender-based classifications
should be subject to "heightened scrutiny" under the
Equal Protection Clause. Sexist laws cannot survive
challenge merely through a rational justification. Since
Virginia cannot offer the "exceedingly persuasive justification" for separate facilities that Ginsburg says the
Constitution demands, VMI cannot continue to exclude women.*

Founded in 1839, VMI is today the sole single sex school among Virginia's 15 public institutions of higher learning. VMI's distinctive mission is to produce "citizen soldiers," men prepared for leadership in civilian life and in military service. VMI pursues this mission through pervasive training of a kind not available anywhere else in Virginia. Assigning prime place to character development, VMI uses an "adversative method" modeled on English public schools and once characteristic of military instruction. The school's graduates leave VMI with heightened comprehension of their capacity to deal with duress and stress, and a large sense of accomplishment for completing the hazardous course. . . .

Neither the goal of producing citizen soldiers nor VMI's implementing methodology is inherently unsuitable to women. And the school's impressive record in producing leaders has made admission desirable to some women. Nevertheless, Virginia has elected to preserve exclusively for men the advantages and opportunities a VMI education affords. . . .

In 1990, prompted by a complaint filed with the Attorney General by a female high school student seeking admission to VMI, the United States sued the Commonwealth of Virginia and VMI, alleging that VMI's exclusively male admission policy violated the Equal Protection Clause of the Fourteenth Amendment. . . .

The District Court ruled in favor of VMI, however, and rejected the equal protection challenge pressed by the United States. . . . There, this Court underscored that a party seeking to uphold government action based on sex must establish an "exceedingly persuasive justification" for the classification. . . .

The Court of Appeals for the Fourth Circuit disagreed and vacated the District Court's judgment. The appellate court held: "The Commonwealth of Virginia has not . . . advanced any state policy by which it can justify its determination, under an announced policy of diversity, to afford VMI's unique type of program to men and not to women."

. . . Remanding the case, the appeals court assigned to Virginia, in the first instance, responsibility for selecting a remedial course. The court suggested these options for the State: Admit women to VMI; establish parallel institutions or programs; or abandon state support, leaving VMI free to pursue its policies as a private institution.

In response to the Fourth Circuit's ruling, Virginia proposed a parallel program for women: Virginia Women's Institute for Leadership (VWIL). The 4 year, state sponsored undergraduate program would be located at Mary Baldwin College, a private liberal arts school for women, and would be open, initially, to about 25 to 30 students. Although VWIL would share VMI's mission—to produce "citizen soldiers"—the VWIL program would differ, as does Mary Baldwin College, from VMI in academic offerings, methods of education, and financial resources. . . .

Virginia returned to the District Court seeking approval of its proposed remedial plan, and the court decided the plan met the requirements of the Equal Protection Clause. . . .

A divided Court of Appeals affirmed the District Court's judgment. . . .

. . . Exclusion of "men at Mary Baldwin College and women at VMI," the court said, was essential to Virginia's purpose, for without such exclusion, the State could not "accomplish [its] objective of providing single gender education."

. . . The court . . . added another inquiry, a decisive test it called "substantive comparability." The key question, the court said, was whether men at VMI and women at VWIL would obtain "substantively comparable benefits at their institution or through other means offered by the [S]tate." Although the appeals court recognized that the VWIL degree "lacks the historical benefit and prestige" of a VMI degree, it nevertheless found the educational opportunities at the two schools "sufficiently comparable." . . .

The cross-petitions in this case present two ultimate issues. First, does Virginia's exclusion of women from the educational opportunities provided by VMI—extraordinary opportunities for military training and civilian leadership development—deny to women "capable of all of the individual activities required of VMI cadets," the equal protection of the laws guaranteed by the Fourteenth Amendment? Second, if VMI's "unique" situation—as Virginia's sole single sex public institution of higher education—offends the Constitution's equal protection principle, what is the remedial requirement? . . .

Today's skeptical scrutiny of official action denying rights or opportunities based on sex responds to volumes of history. As a plurality of this Court acknowledged a generation ago, "our Nation has had a long and unfortunate history of sex discrimination." Through a century plus three decades and more of that history, women did not count among voters composing "We the People"; not until 1920 did women gain a constitutional right to the franchise. And for a half century thereafter, it remained the prevailing doctrine that government, both federal and state, could withhold from women opportunities accorded men so long as any "basis in reason" could be conceived for the discrimination. . . .

In 1971, for the first time in our Nation's history, this Court ruled in favor of a woman who complained that her State had denied her the equal protection of its laws. Since

*Reed*, the Court has repeatedly recognized that neither federal nor state government acts compatibly with the equal protection principle when a law or official policy denies to women, simply because they are women, full citizenship stature— equal opportunity to aspire, achieve, participate in and contribute to society based on their individual talents and capacities. . . .

Without equating gender classifications, for all purposes, to classifications based on race or national origin, the Court, in post-*Reed* decisions, has carefully inspected official action that closes a door or denies opportunity to women (or to men). To summarize the Court's current directions for cases of official classification based on gender: Focusing on the differential treatment or denial of opportunity for which relief is sought, the reviewing court must determine whether the proffered justification is "exceedingly persuasive." The burden of justification is demanding and it rests entirely on the State. . . .

"Inherent differences" between men and women, we have come to appreciate, remain cause for celebration, but not for denigration of the members of either sex or for artificial constraints on an individual's opportunity. Sex classifications . . . may not be used, as they once were, to create or perpetuate the legal, social, and economic inferiority of women.

Measuring the record in this case against the review standard just described, we conclude that Virginia has shown no "exceedingly persuasive justification" for excluding all women from the citizen soldier training afforded by VMI. We therefore affirm the Fourth Circuit's initial judgment, which held that Virginia had violated the Fourteenth Amendment's Equal Protection Clause. Because the remedy proffered by Virginia—the Mary Baldwin VWIL program—does not cure the constitutional violation, i.e., it does not provide equal opportunity, we reverse the Fourth Circuit's final judgment in this case. . . .

. . . Virginia asserts two justifications in defense of VMI's exclusion of women. First, the Commonwealth contends, "single sex education provides important educational benefits," and the option of single sex education contributes to "diversity in educational approaches." Second, the Commonwealth argues, "the unique VMI method of character development and leadership training," the school's adversative approach, would have to be modified were VMI to admit women. We consider these two justifications in turn.

Single sex education affords pedagogical benefits to at least some students, Virginia emphasizes, and that reality is uncontested in this litigation. Similarly, it is not disputed that diversity among public educational institutions can serve the public good. But Virginia has not shown that VMI was established, or has been maintained, with a view to . . . diversifying, by its categorical exclusion of women, educational opportunities within the Commonwealth. . . .

Virginia describes the current absence of public single sex higher education for women as "an historical anomaly." But the historical record indicates action more deliberate than anomalous: First, protection of women against higher education; next, schools for women far from equal in resources and stature to schools for men; finally, conversion of the separate schools to coeducation. The state legislature, prior to the advent of this controversy, had repealed "[a]ll Virginia statutes requiring individual institutions to admit only men or women." And in 1990, an official commission, "legislatively established to chart the future goals of higher education in Virginia," reaffirmed the policy "of affording broad access" while maintaining "autonomy and diversity." Significantly, the Commission reported:

"Because colleges and universities provide opportunities for students to develop values and learn from role models, it is extremely important that they deal with faculty, staff, and students without regard to sex, race, or ethnic origin."

This statement, the Court of Appeals observed, "is the only explicit one that we have found in the record in which the Commonwealth has expressed itself with respect to gender distinctions." . . .

In sum, we find no persuasive evidence in this record that VMI's male only admission policy "is in furtherance of a state policy of 'diversity.'" . . . A purpose genuinely to advance an array of educational options, as the Court of Appeals recognized, is not served by VMI's historic and constant plan—a plan to "affor[d] a unique educational benefit only to males." However "liberally" this plan serves the State's sons, it makes no provision whatever for her daughters. That is not *equal* protection.

Virginia next argues that VMI's adversative method of training provides educational benefits that cannot be made available, unmodified, to women. Alterations to accommodate women would necessarily be "radical," so "drastic," Virginia asserts, as to transform, indeed "destroy," VMI's program. . . .

. . . [I]t is uncontested that women's admission would require accommodations, primarily in arranging housing assignments and physical training programs for female cadets. It is also undisputed, however, that "the VMI methodology could be used to educate women." The District Court even allowed that some women may prefer it to the methodology a women's college might pursue . . . and "some women," the expert testimony established, "are capable of all of the individual activities required of VMI cadets." The parties, furthermore, agree that "some women can meet the physical standards [VMI] now impose[s] on men." In sum, as the Court of Appeals stated, "neither the goal of producing citizen soldiers," VMI's *raison d'être*, "nor VMI's implementing methodology is inherently unsuitable to women."

In support of its initial judgment for Virginia, a judgment rejecting all equal protection objections presented by the United States, the District Court made "findings" on "gender based developmental differences." These "findings" restate the opinions of Virginia's expert witnesses, opinions about typically male or typically female "tendencies." . . .

The United States does not challenge any expert witness estimation on average capacities or preferences of men and women. Instead, the United States emphasizes that time and again since this Court's turning point decision in *Reed* v. *Reed*, we have cautioned reviewing courts to take a "hard look" at generalizations or "tendencies" of the kind pressed by Virginia, and relied upon by the District Court. State actors controlling gates to opportunity, we have instructed, may not exclude qualified individuals based on "fixed notions concerning the roles and abilities of males and females." . . .

. . . Education, to be sure, is not a "one size fits all" business. The issue, however, is not whether "women—or men— should be forced to attend VMI"; rather, the question is whether the State can constitutionally deny to women who have the will and capacity, the training and attendant opportunities that VMI uniquely affords.

The notion that admission of women would downgrade VMI's stature, destroy the adversative system and, with it, even the school, is a judgment hardly proved, a prediction hardly different from other "self fulfilling prophec[ies]," once routinely used to deny rights or opportunities. . . .

Women's successful entry into the federal military academies, and their participation in the Nation's military forces, indicate that Virginia's fears for the future of VMI may not be solidly grounded. The State's justification for excluding all women from "citizen soldier" training for which some are qualified, in any event, cannot rank as "exceedingly persuasive," as we have explained and applied that standard. . . .

The Commonwealth's misunderstanding and, in turn, the District Court's, is apparent from VMI's mission: to produce "citizen soldiers," individuals . . . "imbued with love of learning, confident in the functions and attitudes of leadership, possessing a high sense of public service, advocates of the American democracy and free enterprise system, and ready . . . to defend their country in time of national peril." Surely that goal is great enough to accommodate women, who today count as citizens in our American democracy equal in stature to men. Just as surely, the Commonwealth's great goal is not substantially advanced by women's categorical exclusion, in total disregard of their individual merit, from the Commonwealth's premier "citizen soldier" corps. Virginia, in sum, "has fallen far short of establishing the 'exceedingly persuasive justification'" that must be the solid base for any gender defined classification.

In the second phase of the litigation, Virginia presented its remedial plan—maintain VMI as a male only college and create VWIL as a separate program for women. . . .

A remedial decree, this Court has said, must closely fit the constitutional violation; it must be shaped to place persons unconstitutionally denied an opportunity or advantage in "the position they would have occupied in the absence of [discrimination]." . . . The constitutional violation in this case is the categorical exclusion of women from an extraordinary educational opportunity afforded men. A proper remedy for an unconstitutional exclusion, we have explained, aims to "eliminate [so far as possible] the discriminatory effects of the past" and to "bar like discrimination in the future."

Virginia chose not to eliminate, but to leave untouched, VMI's exclusionary policy. For women only, however, Virginia proposed a separate program, different in kind from VMI and unequal in tangible and intangible facilities. . . . Virginia described VWIL as a "parallel program," and asserted that VWIL shares VMI's mission of producing "citizen soldiers." . . .

VWIL affords women no opportunity to experience the rigorous military training for which VMI is famed. . . . Instead, the VWIL program "deemphasize[s]" military education, and uses a "cooperative method" of education "which reinforces self-esteem." . . .

Virginia maintains that these methodological differences are "justified pedagogically," based on "important differences between men and women in learning and developmental needs," "psychological and sociological differences" Virginia describes as "real" and "not stereotypes." . . .

As earlier stated, . . . generalizations about "the way women are," estimates of what is appropriate for *most women*, no longer justify denying opportunity to women whose talent and capacity place them outside the average description. . . .

In contrast to the generalizations about women on which Virginia rests, we note again these dispositive realties: VMI's "implementing methodology" is not "inherently unsuitable to women"; "some women . . . do well under [the] adversative model"; "some women, at least, would want to attend [VMI] if they had the opportunity"; "some women are capable of all of the individual activities required of VMI cadets," and "can meet the physical standards [VMI] now impose[s] on men." It is on behalf of these women that the United States has instituted this suit, and it is for them that a remedy must be crafted, a remedy that will end their exclusion from a state supplied educational opportunity for which they are fit, a decree that will "bar like discrimination in the future."

In myriad respects other than military training, VWIL does not qualify as VMI's equal. . . . VWIL's student body, faculty, course offerings, and facilities hardly match VMI's. Nor can the VWIL graduate anticipate the benefits associated with VMI's 157-year history, the school's prestige, and its influential alumni network. . . .

Virginia, in sum, while maintaining VMI for men only, has failed to provide any "comparable single gender women's institution." Instead, the Commonwealth has created a VWIL program fairly appraised as a "pale shadow" of VMI in terms of the range of curricular choices and faculty stature, funding, prestige, alumni support and influence. . . .

. . . [W]e rule here that Virginia has not shown substantial equality in the separate educational opportunities the State supports at VWIL and VMI. . . .

We have earlier described the deferential review in which the Court of Appeals engaged a brand of review inconsistent with the more exacting standard our precedent requires. . . . Recognizing that it had extracted from our decisions a test yielding "little or no scrutiny of the effect of a classification directed at [single gender education]," the Court of Appeals devised another test, a "substantive comparability" inquiry and proceeded to find that new test satisfied.

The Fourth Circuit plainly erred in exposing Virginia's VWIL plan to a deferential analysis, for "all gender based classifications today" warrant "heightened scrutiny." Valuable as VWIL may prove for students who seek the program offered, Virginia's remedy affords no cure at all for the opportunities and advantages withheld from women who want a VMI education and can make the grade. In sum, Virginia's remedy does not match the constitutional violation; the State has shown no "exceedingly persuasive justification" for withholding from women qualified for the experience premier training of the kind VMI affords. . . .

VMI, too, offers an educational opportunity no other Virginia institution provides, and the school's "prestige"—associated with its success in developing "citizen soldiers"—is unequaled. Virginia has closed this facility to its daughters and, instead, has devised for them a "parallel program," with a faculty less impressively credentialed and less well paid, more limited course offerings, fewer opportunities for military training and for scientific specialization. VMI, beyond question, "possesses to a far greater degree" than the VWIL program "those qualities which are incapable of objective measurement but which make for greatness in a . . . school." . . . Women seeking and fit for a VMI quality education cannot be offered anything less, under the State's obligation to afford them genuinely equal protection.

A prime part of the history of our Constitution, historian Richard Morris recounted, is the story of the extension of constitutional rights and protections to people once ignored or excluded. VMI's story continued as our comprehension of "We the People" expanded. There is no reason to believe that the admission of women capable of all the activities required of VMI cadets would destroy the Institute rather than enhance its capacity to serve the "more perfect Union." . . .

========

For the reasons stated, the initial judgment of the Court of Appeals is affirmed, the final judgment of the Court of Appeals is reversed, and the case is remanded for further proceedings consistent with this opinion.

*It is so ordered.*

# Dissenting Opinion in *Ledbetter v. Goodyear Tire and Rubber Co., Inc.* (2007)

*Lilly Ledbetter was a supervisor at the Goodyear Tire Company, where she worked for nineteen years. She was unique at the plant for two reasons. First, she was one of the only women—and sometimes the only woman—in her position. Second, she was paid less than everyone else in her job and had been for years. Upon learning the extent of the pay disparities, she made a formal pay discrimination complaint to the Equal Employment Opportunities Commission under Title VII of the Civil Rights Act. When her case reached the Supreme Court, Justice Samuel Alito wrote that Ledbetter was not entitled to relief, since she did not file her complaint within 180 days of the discriminatory pay decision, as the statute required.*

*Justice Ginsburg dissented. In this opinion, she argues that the majority's formalistic emphasis on the initial 180-day limit undermines the true purpose of the bill: ensuring pay equity for women. Gender-based pay discrimination, she says, cannot just be categorized into "discrete" acts. Ledbetter faced ongoing discrimination throughout her career, with each smaller raise she was given because she was a woman culminating in a*

> *disparity at the time of filing—a disparity, Ginsburg*
> *argues, that was unacceptable in an equal society.*
>
> *Ginsburg's insistence on rectifying pay discrimina-*
> *tion in a holistic manner did not win the day in Court.*
> *But her fiery dissent became a prime example of how*
> *even in defeat, her ideas have changed the world. Just*
> *two years later, Congress passed the Lilly Ledbetter Fair*
> *Pay Act, overturning the Court's ruling and endorsing*
> *Ginsburg's view that each unequal paycheck counts as a*
> *separate discriminatory act.*

Lilly Ledbetter was a supervisor at Goodyear Tire and Rubber's plant in Gadsden, Alabama, from 1979 until her retirement in 1998. For most of those years, she worked as an area manager, a position largely occupied by men. Initially, Ledbetter's salary was in line with the salaries of men performing substantially similar work. Over time, however, her pay slipped in comparison to the pay of male area managers with equal or less seniority. By the end of 1997, Ledbetter was the only woman working as an area manager and the pay discrepancy between Ledbetter and her 15 male counterparts was stark: Ledbetter was paid $3,727 per month; the lowest paid male area manager received $4,286 per month, the highest paid, $5,236.

Ledbetter launched charges of discrimination before the Equal Employment Opportunity Commission (EEOC) in March 1998. Her formal administrative complaint specified that, in violation of Title VII, Goodyear paid her a discriminatorily low salary because of her sex. That charge was eventually tried to a jury, which found it "more likely than not that [Goodyear] paid [Ledbetter] a[n] unequal salary because of her sex." In accord with the jury's liability determination, the

District Court entered judgment for Ledbetter for backpay and damages, plus counsel fees and costs.

The Court of Appeals for the Eleventh Circuit reversed. Relying on Goodyear's system of annual merit-based raises, the court held that Ledbetter's claim, in relevant part, was time barred. Title VII provides that a charge of discrimination "shall be filed within [180] days after the alleged unlawful employment practice occurred." Ledbetter charged, and proved at trial, that within the 180-day period, her pay was substantially less than the pay of men doing the same work. Further, she introduced evidence sufficient to establish that discrimination against female managers at the Gadsden plant, not performance inadequacies on her part, accounted for the pay differential. That evidence was unavailing, the Eleventh Circuit held, and the Court today agrees, because it was incumbent on Ledbetter to file charges year-by-year, each time Goodyear failed to increase her salary commensurate with the salaries of male peers. . . .

The Court's insistence on immediate contest overlooks common characteristics of pay discrimination. Pay disparities often occur, as they did in Ledbetter's case, in small increments; cause to suspect that discrimination is at work develops only over time. Comparative pay information, moreover, is often hidden from the employee's view. Employers may keep under wraps the pay differentials maintained among supervisors, no less the reasons for those differentials. Small initial discrepancies may not be seen as meet for a federal case, particularly when the employee, trying to succeed in a nontraditional environment, is averse to making waves.

. . . It is only when the disparity becomes apparent and sizable, e.g., through future raises calculated as a percentage of current salaries, that an employee in Ledbetter's situation is likely to comprehend her plight and, therefore, to complain.

Her initial readiness to give her employer the benefit of the doubt should not preclude her from later challenging the then current and continuing payment of a wage depressed on account of her sex.

# I

Title VII proscribes as an "unlawful employment practice" discrimination "against any individual with respect to his compensation . . . because of such individual's race, color, religion, sex, or national origin." An individual seeking to challenge an employment practice under this proscription must file a charge with the EEOC within 180 days "after the alleged unlawful employment practice occurred."

Ledbetter's petition presents a question important to the sound application of Title VII: What activity qualifies as an unlawful employment practice in cases of discrimination with respect to compensation. One answer identifies the pay-setting decision, and that decision alone, as the unlawful practice. Under this view, each particular salary-setting decision is discrete from prior and subsequent decisions, and must be challenged within 180 days on pain of forfeiture. Another response counts both the pay-setting decision and the actual payment of a discriminatory wage as unlawful practices. Under this approach, each payment of a wage or salary infected by sex-based discrimination constitutes an unlawful employment practice; prior decisions, outside the 180-day charge-filing period, are not themselves actionable, but they are relevant in determining the lawfulness of conduct within the period. The Court adopts the first view, but the second is more faithful to precedent, more in tune with the realities of the workplace, and more respectful of Title VII's remedial purpose.

## A

In *Bazemore*, we unanimously held that an employer, the North Carolina Agricultural Extension Service, committed an unlawful employment practice each time it paid black employees less than similarly situated white employees. . . . [W]e reasoned, "[e]ach week's paycheck that delivers less to a black than to a similarly situated white is a wrong actionable under Title VII." Paychecks perpetuating past discrimination, we thus recognized, are actionable not simply because they are "related" to a decision made outside the charge-filing period, but because they discriminate anew each time they issue.

Subsequently, in *Morgan*, we set apart, for purposes of Title VII's timely filing requirement, unlawful employment actions of two kinds: "discrete acts" that are "easy to identify" as discriminatory, and acts that recur and are cumulative in impact. . . .

"[D]ifferent in kind from discrete acts," we made clear, are "claims . . . based on the cumulative effect of individual acts." The *Morgan* decision placed hostile work environment claims in that category. . . . "The unlawful employment practice" in hostile work environment claims, "cannot be said to occur on any particular day. It occurs over a series of days or perhaps years and, in direct contrast to discrete acts, a single act of harassment may not be actionable on its own." The persistence of the discriminatory conduct both indicates that management should have known of its existence and produces a cognizable harm. Because the very nature of the hostile work environment claim involves repeated conduct, "[i]t does not matter, for purposes of the statute, that some of the component acts of the hostile work environment fall outside the statutory time period. . . ." Consequently, although the unlawful conduct began in the past, "a charge may be filed at a later date and still encompass the whole."

Pay disparities, of the kind Ledbetter experienced, have a closer kinship to hostile work environment claims than to charges of a single episode of discrimination. Ledbetter's claim, resembling Morgan's, rested not on one particular paycheck, but on "the cumulative effect of individual acts." She charged insidious discrimination building up slowly but steadily. Initially in line with the salaries of men performing substantially the same work, Ledbetter's salary fell 15 to 40 percent behind her male counterparts only after successive evaluations and percentage-based pay adjustments. Over time, she alleged and proved, the repetition of pay decisions undervaluing her work gave rise to the current discrimination of which she complained. Though component acts fell outside the charge-filing period, with each new paycheck, Goodyear contributed incrementally to the accumulating harm.

## B

The realities of the workplace reveal why the discrimination with respect to compensation that Ledbetter suffered does not fit within the category of singular discrete acts "easy to identify." A worker knows immediately if she is denied a promotion or transfer, if she is fired or refused employment. And promotions, transfers, hirings, and firings are generally public events, known to co-workers. When an employer makes a decision of such open and definitive character, an employee can immediately seek out an explanation and evaluate it for pretext. Compensation disparities, in contrast, are often hidden from sight. . . . Tellingly, as the record in this case bears out, Goodyear kept salaries confidential; employees had only limited access to information regarding their colleagues' earnings.

The problem of concealed pay discrimination is particularly acute where the disparity arises not because the female employee is flatly denied a raise but because male counterparts are given larger raises. Having received a pay increase, the female employee is unlikely to discern at once that she has experienced an adverse employment decision. She may have little reason even to suspect discrimination until a pattern develops incrementally and she ultimately becomes aware of the disparity. Even if an employee suspects that the reason for a comparatively low raise is not performance but sex (or another protected ground), the amount involved may seem too small, or the employer's intent too ambiguous, to make the issue immediately actionable—or winnable. . . .

## C

In light of the significant differences between pay disparities and discrete employment decisions of the type identified in *Morgan*, the cases on which the Court relies hold no sway. . . . No repetitive, cumulative discriminatory employment practice was at issue in either case.

*Lorance* is also inapposite, for, in this Court's view, it too involved a one-time discrete act: the adoption of a new seniority system that "had its genesis in sex discrimination." The Court's extensive reliance on *Lorance*, moreover, is perplexing for that decision is no longer effective: In the 1991 Civil Rights Act, Congress superseded *Lorance*'s holding. . . .

Until today, in the more than 15 years since Congress amended Title VII, the Court had not once relied upon *Lorance*. It is mistaken to do so now. . . . Congress never intended to immunize forever discriminatory pay differentials unchallenged within 180 days of their adoption. This assessment gains weight when one comprehends that even a relatively minor pay disparity will expand exponentially over an employee's working life if raises are set as a percentage of prior pay.

A clue to congressional intent can be found in Title VII's backpay provision. The statute expressly provides that backpay may be awarded for a period of up to two years before the discrimination charge is filed. This prescription indicates that Congress contemplated challenges to pay discrimination commencing before, but continuing into, the 180-day filing period. . . .

# II

The Court asserts that treating pay discrimination as a discrete act, limited to each particular pay-setting decision, is necessary to "protec[t] employers from the burden of defending claims arising from employment decisions that are long past." But the discrimination of which Ledbetter complained is *not* long past. As she alleged, and as the jury found, Goodyear continued to treat Ledbetter differently because of sex each pay period, with mounting harm. Allowing employees to challenge discrimination "that extend[s] over long periods of time," into the charge-filing period, we have previously explained, "does not leave employers defenseless" against unreasonable or prejudicial delay. Employers disadvantaged by such delay may raise various defenses. . . .

In a last-ditch argument, the Court asserts that this dissent would allow a plaintiff to sue on a single decision made 20 years ago "even if the employee had full knowledge of all the circumstances relating to the . . . decision at the time it was made." It suffices to point out that the defenses just noted would make such a suit foolhardy. No sensible judge would tolerate such inexcusable neglect.

Ledbetter, the Court observes, dropped an alternative remedy she could have pursued: Had she persisted in pressing her claim under the Equal Pay Act of 1963, she would not have encountered a time bar. Notably, the EPA provides no relief when the pay discrimination charged is based on race, religion, national origin, age, or disability. Thus, in truncating the Title VII rule this Court announced in *Bazemore*, the Court does not disarm female workers from achieving redress for unequal pay, but it does impede racial and other minorities from gaining similar relief.

Furthermore, the difference between the EPA's prohibition against paying unequal wages and Title VII's ban on discrimination with regard to compensation is not as large as the Court's opinion might suggest. The key distinction is that Title VII requires a showing of intent. In practical effect, "if the trier of fact is in equipoise about whether the wage differential is motivated by gender discrimination," Title VII compels a verdict for the employer, while the EPA compels a verdict for the plaintiff. In this case, Ledbetter carried the burden of persuading the jury that the pay disparity she suffered was attributable to intentional sex discrimination.

# III

To show how far the Court has strayed from interpretation of Title VII with fidelity to the Act's core purpose, I return to the evidence Ledbetter presented at trial. Ledbetter proved to the jury the following: She was a member of a protected class; she performed work substantially equal to work of the dominant class (men); she was compensated less for that work; and the disparity was attributable to gender-based discrimination.

Specifically, Ledbetter's evidence demonstrated that her current pay was discriminatorily low due to a long series of decisions reflecting Goodyear's pervasive discrimination against women managers in general and Ledbetter in particular. Ledbetter's former supervisor, for example, admitted to the jury that Ledbetter's pay, during a particular one-year period, fell below Goodyear's minimum threshold for her position. Although Goodyear claimed the pay disparity was due to poor performance, the supervisor acknowledged that Ledbetter received a "Top Performance Award" in 1996. The jury also heard testimony that another supervisor—who evaluated Ledbetter in 1997 and whose evaluation led to her most recent raise denial—was openly biased against women. And two women who had previously worked as managers at the plant told the jury they had been subject to pervasive discrimination and were paid less than their male counterparts. One was paid less than the men she supervised. Ledbetter herself testified about the discriminatory animus conveyed to her by plant officials. Toward the end of her career, for instance, the plant manager told Ledbetter that the "plant did not need women, that [women] didn't help it, [and] caused problems." After weighing all the evidence, the jury found for Ledbetter, concluding that the pay disparity was due to intentional discrimination.

Yet, under the Court's decision, the discrimination Ledbetter proved is not redressable under Title VII. Each and every pay decision she did not immediately challenge wiped the slate clean. Consideration may not be given to the cumulative effect of a series of decisions that, together, set her pay well below that of every male area manager. Knowingly carrying past pay discrimination forward must be treated as lawful conduct. Ledbetter may not be compensated for the lower pay she was in fact receiving when she complained to the EEOC. . . . The Court's approbation of these consequences is totally at odds with the robust protection against workplace discrimination Congress intended Title VII to secure.

This is not the first time the Court has ordered a cramped interpretation of Title VII, incompatible with the statute's broad remedial purpose. Once again, the ball is in Congress' court. As in 1991, the Legislature may act to correct this Court's parsimonious reading of Title VII.

===

For the reasons stated, I would hold that Ledbetter's claim is not time barred and would reverse the Eleventh Circuit's judgment.

# *Part II*

# REPRODUCTIVE FREEDOM

The decision whether or not to bear a child is central to a woman's life, to her well-being and dignity. It is a decision she must make for herself. When Government controls that decision for her, she is being treated as less than a fully adult human responsible for her own choices. Abortion prohibition by the State . . . controls women and denies them full autonomy and full equality with men.

—RUTH BADER GINSBURG,
SENATE CONFIRMATION HEARING, JULY 21, 1993

# Brief for the Petitioner in *Struck v. Secretary of Defense* (1972)

*When modern readers think of reproductive freedom and the Supreme Court, they likely think of* Roe v. Wade. *Justice Ginsburg thinks an alternate path could have better secured the right to an abortion. She has said that she would have preferred the major abortion rights case to be* Struck v. Secretary of Defense. *To Ginsburg,* Roe's *focus on the right to privacy and the doctor-patient relationship was important but did not on its own provide the strongest constitutional basis for the right to an abortion. In the following brief, she argues that abortion rights should be an extension of the freedoms and opportunities equal to those that women are guaranteed through the Fifth and Fourteenth Amendments' Due Process and Equal Protection Clauses.*

## STATEMENT OF THE CASE

Captain Susan R. Struck, the petitioner, is a career officer in the United States Air Force. She entered on active duty as a commissioned officer on April 8, 1967, and has served on active duty continuously since that date. On September 14,

1970, in Vietnam, it was determined that the petitioner was pregnant. . . .

[I]n a waiver application dated October 9, 1970, Captain Struck declared her intention to place her child for adoption immediately after birth; . . . The board of officers found that petitioner was pregnant and recommended her separation from the Air Force pursuant to Air Force Regulation 36-12(40), which then mandated discharge action upon determination that a woman officer is pregnant. On October 26, 1970, the Secretary of the Air Force . . . directed that Captain Struck be discharged as soon as possible. . . .

On February 1, 1971, District Judge Goodwin entered his decision, holding the regulation applied to petitioner to be constitutional and granting the defendants' motion to dismiss the complaint. . . .

On November 15, 1971, a panel of the Court of Appeals for the Ninth Circuit unanimously affirmed the district court's order. . . .

# ARGUMENT

## I

Petitioner, a career officer who at all times has maintained an excellent service record, has been ordered discharged because she became pregnant and gave birth to a living child. The regulation invoked against her applies automatically. It declares a pregnant officer, who does not promptly abort the fetus, unfit for service. Thus it precludes petitioner's continued pursuit of her chosen Air Force career despite the excellent quality of her work. . . .

The central question raised in this case is whether the Air

Force, consistent with the equal protection principle inherent in the due process clause of the fifth amendment, may call for immediate discharge of pregnant women officers (whether detection of pregnancy occurs at 8 days or 8 months), unless pregnancy terminates soon after detection, while granting sick leave for all other physical conditions occasioning a period of temporary disability. It is petitioner's position that this distinction reflects arbitrary notions of woman's place wholly at odds with contemporary legislative and judicial recognition that individual potential must not be restrained, nor equal opportunity limited, by law-sanctioned stereotypical prejudgments. Captain Struck seeks no favors or special protection. She simply asks to be judged on the basis of her individual capacities and qualifications, and not on the basis of characteristics assumed to typify pregnant women.

## II

"Nobody—and this includes Judges Solomonic or life tenured—has yet seen a pregnant male." Does disadvantaged treatment of women based on a physical condition no man can experience constitute sex discrimination? Jurists whose perspective reaches beyond the observation that "it can't happen to a man," have answered emphatically "Yes."

Sex discrimination exists when all or a defined class of women (or men) are subjected to disadvantaged treatment based on stereotypical assumptions that operate to foreclose opportunity based on individual merit. . . .

The Air Force regulation directing Captain Struck's discharge is a blatant example of stereotypical prejudgment that shuts out consideration of individual capacities. The regulation singles out pregnancy, a physical condition unique to women involving a normally brief period of disability, as cause for immediate involuntary discharge. No other physical condition occasioning a period of temporary disability, whether affecting a man or a woman, is similarly treated. . . .

### A

Pregnancy regulations distinctly less severe than the Air Force involuntary discharge requirement at issue here have failed to survive judicial scrutiny. The trend of judicial opinion is clear: regulations applicable to pregnancy more onerous than regulations applicable to other temporary physical conditions discriminate invidiously on the basis of sex. . . .

Because pregnancy, though unique to women, is like other medical conditions, the failure to treat it as such amounts to discrimination which is without rational basis, and therefore is violative of the equal protection clause of the Fourteenth Amendment.

It is the very inflexibility of the Board's policy which casts a light of dubious constitutionality about its regulations. . . . While it may be quite true that some women are incapacitated by pregnancy . . . , to say that this is true of all women is to define that half of our population in stereotypical terms and to deal with them artificially. Sexual stereotypes are no less invidious than racial or religious ones. Any rule by an employer that seeks to deal with all pregnant employees in an identical fashion is dehumanizing to the individual woman involved and is by its very nature arbitrary and discriminatory. . . .

*Ginsburg is making an obvious yet often overlooked point: abortion regulations are regulations that can apply only to women, meaning that they draw distinctions based on gender. Without a compelling government rationale for those distinctions, they should be impermissible. Generalizations based on what men think pregnant women are like clearly are not strong enough reasons. Ginsburg then has to show the harm that these generalizations posed, both in working against a growing societal consensus toward gender equality and in diminishing the opportunities made available to women.*

## III

### . . . B

In very recent years, a new appreciation of women's place has been generated in the United States. Activated by feminists of both sexes, legislatures and courts have begun to recognize and respond to the subordinate position of women in our society and the second-class status our institutions historically have imposed upon them. The heightened national awareness that equal opportunity for men and women is a matter of simple justice has led to significant reform. . . .

The significant changes that have occurred in society's attitudes toward equal opportunity for men and women should yield a deeper appreciation of the premise underlying the "suspect classification" doctrine: . . . it is presumptively impermissible to distinguish on the basis of congenital and unalterable traits of birth over which the individual has no control and for which he or she should not be penalized. Such conditions include not only race, lineage and alienage, criteria already declared "suspect" by this Court, but include as well the sex of the individual.

No longer shackled by decisions reflecting social attitudes and economic conditions of an earlier era, enlightened judges in both federal and state courts are becoming increasingly skeptical of lines drawn or sanctioned by governmental authority on the basis of sex. . . .

. . . What differentiates sex from non-suspect statuses, such as intelligence or physical disability, and aligns it with the recognized suspect classifications is that the characteristic frequently bears no relation to ability to perform or contribute to society. . . . The result is that the whole class is relegated to an inferior legal status without regard to the capabilities or characteristics of its individual members. . . .

Laws which disable women from full participation in the political, business and economic arenas are often characterized as "protective" and beneficial. Those same laws applied to racial or ethnic minorities would readily be recognized as invidious and impermissible. The pedestal upon which women have been placed has all too often, upon closer inspection, been revealed as a cage. We conclude that the sexual classifications are properly treated as suspect, particularly when those classifications are made with respect to a fundamental interest such as employment. . . .

I.

. . . Heading the list of arbitrary barriers that have plagued women seeking equal opportunity is disadvantaged treatment based on their unique childbearing function. This reality has been obscured by the historical tendency of jurists to regard any discrimination in the treatment of women as "benignly in their favor." Summary dismissal of, or forced, unpaid leave for pregnant women, still widespread and until very recently the common pattern, continues to be rationalized as "protective." In fact, such practices operate as "built-in headwinds" that drastically curtail women's opportunities.

Unquestionably, as petitioner's experience illustrates, many women are capable of working effectively during pregnancy and require only a brief period of absence immediately before and after childbirth. Regulations that disregard this reality and "protect" all women who are pregnant, that is, deny them the opportunity to work, without regard to individual circumstances, have in practice deprived working women of the protection they most need: protection of their right to work to support themselves and, in many cases, their families as well. . . .

For a large segment of the female labor force, gainful employment is dictated by economic necessity. Earnings for this group are hardly "pin money"; their jobs are often the sole source of income for themselves and, in many cases, their dependent children. Even where husbands are present and employed, the wife's earnings frequently are necessary to keep the family above a bare subsistence level. Discharge for pregnancy, attended by termination of income and fringe benefits, and denial of the right to return after childbirth, disables these women far more than their temporary physical condition.

For the more fortunate woman, for whom work is not dictated by economic necessity, mandatory pregnancy discharge reinforces societal pressure to relinquish career aspirations for a hearth-centered existence. . . .

## IV

The discriminatory treatment required by the challenged regulation, barring pregnant women and mothers from continued service in the Air Force, reflects the discredited notion that a woman who becomes pregnant is not fit for duty, but should be confined at home to await childbirth and thereafter devote herself to child care. Imposition of this outmoded standard upon petitioner unconstitutionally encroaches upon her right to privacy in the conduct of her personal life.

Individual privacy with respect to procreation and intimate personal relations is a right firmly embedded in this nation's tradition and in the precedent of this Court. . . .

The Air Force regulation applied to petitioner substantially infringes upon her right to sexual privacy, and her autonomy in deciding "whether to bear . . . a child." Unlike the situation most frequently presented in current cases involving these rights, the regulation here in question does not prohibit reproduction control. On the contrary, respondents assert that the purpose of the regulation is to "encourage" such control. But when the "encouragement" is directed at females only and takes the form of a stern prohibition—women in the Air Force shall not bear children—the woman's right to privacy and autonomy is invidiously curtailed. Her "choice" operates in one direction only. If she wishes to continue her Air Force career, she must not give birth to a child.

Significantly, men in the Air Force are not "encouraged," on pain of discharge, to use contraceptives and avoid fatherhood. . . . Yet if the purpose of the regulation is to "encourage the use of contraceptives" men and women should be subject to the same restrictions. But the plain fact is that no regulation discourages men in the Air Force, whether married or single, from fathering children. If a man and a woman, both Captains in the Air Force, conceive a child, the man is free to continue his service career, but the woman is subject to involuntary discharge.

Thus the proposition that there is a compelling governmental interest in adopting rules to deter pregnancies thinly veils the underlying concern: parenthood among servicemen is not deterred, indeed additional benefits are provided to encourage men who become fathers to remain in service. Parenthood among servicewomen, on the other hand, is to be prevented. Pregnancy, whether planned, accidental or the result of contraceptive failure, results, under the regulation applied to petitioner, in involuntary discharge, unless the pregnancy is promptly terminated. A man serves in the Air Force with no unwarranted governmental intrusion into the matter of his sexual privacy or his decision whether to beget a child. The woman serves subject to "regulation"; her pursuit of an Air Force career requires that she decide not to bear a child. . . .

*Ginsburg's powerful argument in defense of abortion as an equality issue has been compelling to scholars. It has not, however, entered the Court's mainstream jurisprudence. That's largely because the Supreme Court never decided the case. Captain Struck and the Air Force reached a settlement before the Court heard the case, with Captain Struck allowed to keep her position.*

# Dissenting Opinion in
## *Gonzales v. Carhart* **(2007)**

Roe v. Wade, *decided in 1973, established a constitutional right to have an abortion within the first trimester of a pregnancy, grounded in the right to privacy. Nineteen years later in* Planned Parenthood v. Casey, *the Court reaffirmed the* Roe *ruling but narrowed it: now the right to an abortion would still be guaranteed, but laws regulating abortion that did not put an "undue burden" on access to the practice could pass constitutional muster. Congress then passed a law banning nationwide a practice called "intact D&E," which opponents referred to as "partial-birth abortion." No exception for the health of the mother was included, a stark break with* Roe's *focus on doctor-patient consultation. In* Gonzales v. Carhart, *the Supreme Court upheld the Partial-Birth Abortion Act, writing that its ban on only a specific procedure was clear and did not qualify as an "undue burden."*

*Justice Ginsburg's robust dissent calls out the majority for abandoning the precedents in* Roe *and* Casey. *She herself, as we saw in her brief in* Struck, *would have preferred the Court's abortion jurisprudence to focus more on equal protection. But as a justice, a core duty of*

> *her job is to uphold precedent, and she models that com-*
> *mitment in her dissent here, dissecting what she thinks*
> *are the faulty medical arguments the majority put for-*
> *ward. But notably, Ginsburg also references the link*
> *between abortion rights and equality, noting their rela-*
> *tionship to women's autonomy and "equal citizenship*
> *stature." Unlike in* Ledbetter, *where her dissent spurred*
> *congressional response, the Partial-Birth Abortion Act*
> *remains on the books. But her dissent stands as a call for*
> *a defense of the right to an abortion.*

In *Planned Parenthood of Southeastern Pa.* v. *Casey*, the Court declared that "[l]iberty finds no refuge in a jurisprudence of doubt." There was, the Court said, an "imperative" need to dispel doubt as to "the meaning and reach" of the Court's 7-to-2 judgment, rendered nearly two decades earlier in *Roe* v. *Wade*. Responsive to that need, the Court endeavored to pro-vide secure guidance to "[s]tate and federal courts as well as legislatures throughout the Union," by defining "the rights of the woman and the legitimate authority of the State respect-ing the termination of pregnancies by abortion procedures."

Taking care to speak plainly, the *Casey* Court restated and reaffirmed *Roe*'s essential holding. First, the Court addressed the type of abortion regulation permissible prior to fetal via-bility. It recognized "the right of the woman to choose to have an abortion before viability and to obtain it without undue interference from the State." Second, the Court ac-knowledged "the State's power to restrict abortions *after fetal viability*, if the law contains exceptions for pregnancies which endanger the woman's life *or health*." (emphasis added). Third, the Court confirmed that "the State has legitimate interests from the outset of the pregnancy in protecting *the health of the woman* and the life of the fetus that may become a child." (emphasis added).

In reaffirming *Roe*, the *Casey* Court described the centrality of "the decision whether to bear . . . a child," to a woman's "dignity and autonomy," her "personhood" and "destiny," her "conception of . . . her place in society." Of signal importance here, the *Casey* Court stated with unmistakable clarity that state regulation of access to abortion procedures, even after viability, must protect "the health of the woman."

Seven years ago, in *Stenberg* v. *Carhart*, the Court invalidated a Nebraska statute criminalizing the performance of a medical procedure that, in the political arena, has been dubbed "partial-birth abortion." With fidelity to the *Roe-Casey* line of precedent, the Court held the Nebraska statute unconstitutional in part because it lacked the requisite protection for the preservation of a woman's health.

Today's decision is alarming. It refuses to take *Casey* and *Stenberg* seriously. It tolerates, indeed applauds, federal intervention to ban nationwide a procedure found necessary and proper in certain cases by the American College of Obstetricians and Gynecologists (ACOG). It blurs the line, firmly drawn in *Casey*, between previability and postviability abortions. And, for the first time since *Roe*, the Court blesses a prohibition with no exception safeguarding a woman's health.

I dissent from the Court's disposition. Retreating from prior rulings that abortion restrictions cannot be imposed absent an exception safeguarding a woman's health, the Court upholds an Act that surely would not survive under the close scrutiny that previously attended state-decreed limitations on a woman's reproductive choices.

# I

## A

As *Casey* comprehended, at stake in cases challenging abortion restrictions is a woman's "control over her [own] destiny." "There was a time, not so long ago," when women were "regarded as the center of home and family life, with attendant special responsibilities that precluded full and independent legal status under the Constitution." Those views, this Court made clear in *Casey*, "are no longer consistent with our understanding of the family, the individual, or the Constitution." Women, it is now acknowledged, have the talent, capacity, and right "to participate equally in the economic and social life of the Nation." Their ability to realize their full potential, the Court recognized, is intimately connected to "their ability to control their reproductive lives." Thus, legal challenges to undue restrictions on abortion procedures do not seek to vindicate some generalized notion of privacy; rather, they center on a woman's autonomy to determine her life's course, and thus to enjoy equal citizenship stature.

In keeping with this comprehension of the right to reproductive choice, the Court has consistently required that laws regulating abortion, at any stage of pregnancy and in all cases, safeguard a woman's health. . . .

> "The word 'necessary' in *Casey*'s phrase 'necessary, in appropriate medical judgment, for the preservation of the life or health of the [pregnant woman],' cannot refer to an absolute necessity or to absolute proof. . . .

*Casey*'s words 'appropriate medical judgment' must embody the judicial need to tolerate responsible differences of medical opinion. . . ."

## B

In 2003, a few years after our ruling in *Stenberg*, Congress passed the Partial-Birth Abortion Ban Act—without an exception for women's health. The congressional findings on which the Partial-Birth Abortion Ban Act rests do not withstand inspection, as the lower courts have determined and this Court is obliged to concede. . . .

## C

In contrast to Congress, the District Courts made findings after full trials at which all parties had the opportunity to present their best evidence. . . .

During the District Court trials, "numerous" "extraordinarily accomplished" and "very experienced" medical experts explained that, in certain circumstances and for certain women, intact D&E is safer than alternative procedures and necessary to protect women's health. . . .

Based on thoroughgoing review of the trial evidence and the congressional record, each of the District Courts to consider the issue rejected Congress' findings as unreasonable and not supported by the evidence. The trial courts concluded, in contrast to Congress' findings, that "significant medical authority supports the proposition that in some circumstances, [intact D&E] is the safest procedure."

The District Courts' findings merit this Court's respect. Today's opinion supplies no reason to reject those findings. Nevertheless, despite the District Courts' appraisal of the weight of the evidence, and in undisguised conflict with *Stenberg*, the Court asserts that the Partial-Birth Abortion Ban Act can survive "when . . . medical uncertainty persists." This assertion is bewildering. Not only does it defy the Court's longstanding precedent affirming the necessity of a health exception, with no carve-out for circumstances of medical uncertainty, it gives short shrift to the records before us, carefully canvassed by the District Courts. Those records indicate that "the majority of highly-qualified experts on the subject believe intact D&E to be the safest, most appropriate procedure under certain circumstances."

The Court acknowledges some of this evidence, but insists that, because some witnesses disagreed with the ACOG and other experts' assessment of risk, the Act can stand. In this insistence, the Court brushes under the rug the District Courts' well-supported findings that the physicians who testified that intact D&E is never necessary to preserve the health of a woman had slim authority for their opinions. . . . Even indulging the assumption that the Government witnesses were equally qualified to evaluate the relative risks of abortion procedures, their testimony could not erase the "significant medical authority support[ing] the proposition that in some circumstances, [intact D&E] would be the safest procedure."

## II

### A

The Court offers flimsy and transparent justifications for upholding a nationwide ban on intact D&E *sans* any exception to safeguard a women's health. Today's ruling, the Court declares, advances "a premise central to [*Casey*'s] conclusion"— *i.e.*, the Government's "legitimate and substantial interest in preserving and promoting fetal life." But the Act scarcely furthers that interest: The law saves not a single fetus from destruction, for it targets only a *method* of performing abortion. And surely the statute was not designed to protect the lives or health of pregnant women. In short, the Court upholds a law that, while doing nothing to "preserv[e] . . . fetal life," bars a woman from choosing intact D&E although her doctor "reasonably believes [that procedure] will best protect [her]." . . .

Ultimately, the Court admits that "moral concerns" are at work, concerns that could yield prohibitions on any abortion. Notably, the concerns expressed are untethered to any ground genuinely serving the Government's interest in preserving life. By allowing such concerns to carry the day and case, overriding fundamental rights, the Court dishonors our precedent.

Revealing in this regard, the Court invokes an antiabortion shibboleth for which it concededly has no reliable evidence: Women who have abortions come to regret their choices, and consequently suffer from "[s]evere depression and loss of esteem." Because of women's fragile emotional state and because of the "bond of love the mother has for her child," the Court worries, doctors may withhold information about the nature of the intact D&E procedure. The solution the Court approves, then, is *not* to require doctors to inform women, accurately and adequately, of the different procedures and their attendant risks. Instead, the Court deprives women of the right to make an autonomous choice, even at the expense of their safety.

This way of thinking reflects ancient notions about women's place in the family and under the Constitution—ideas that have long since been discredited. . . .

Though today's majority may regard women's feelings on the matter as "self-evident," this Court has repeatedly confirmed that "[t]he destiny of the woman must be shaped . . . on her own conception of her spiritual imperatives and her place in society."

## B . . .

One wonders how long a line that saves no fetus from destruction will hold in face of the Court's "moral concerns." The Court's hostility to the right *Roe* and *Casey* secured is not concealed. Throughout, the opinion refers to obstetrician-gynecologists and surgeons who perform abortions not by the titles of their medical specialties, but by the pejorative label "abortion doctor." A fetus is described as an "unborn child," and as a "baby," second-trimester, previability abortions are referred to as "late-term," and the reasoned medical judgments of highly trained doctors are dismissed as "preferences" motivated by "mere convenience." Instead of the heightened scrutiny we have previously applied, the Court determines that a "rational" ground is enough to uphold the Act. And, most troubling, *Casey*'s principles, confirming the continuing vitality of "the essential holding of *Roe*," are merely "assume[d]" for the moment, rather than "retained" or "reaffirmed."

# III

## A

Without attempting to distinguish *Stenberg* and earlier decisions, the majority asserts that the Act survives review because respondents have not shown that the ban on intact D&E would be unconstitutional "in a large fraction of relevant cases." But *Casey* makes clear that, in determining whether any restriction poses an undue burden on a "large fraction" of women, the relevant class is *not* "all women," nor "all pregnant women," nor even all women "seeking abortions." Rather, a provision restricting access to abortion, "must be judged by reference to those [women] for whom it is an actual rather than an irrelevant restriction." Thus the absence of a health exception burdens *all* women for whom it is relevant—women who, in the judgment of their doctors, require an intact D&E because other procedures would place their health at risk. It makes no sense to conclude that this facial challenge fails because respondents have not shown that a health exception is necessary for a large fraction of second-trimester abortions, including those for which a health exception is unnecessary: The very purpose of a health *exception* is to protect women in *exceptional* cases.

## B

If there is anything at all redemptive to be said of today's opinion, it is that the Court is not willing to foreclose entirely a constitutional challenge to the Act. "The Act is open," the Court states, "to a proper as-applied challenge in a discrete case." But the Court offers no clue on what a "proper" lawsuit might look like. . . . Surely the Court cannot mean that no suit may be brought until a woman's health is immediately jeopardized by the ban on intact D&E. A woman "suffer[ing] from medical complications" needs access to the medical procedure at once and cannot wait for the judicial process to unfold. . . .

The Court's allowance only of an "as-applied challenge in

a discrete case" jeopardizes women's health and places doctors in an untenable position. Even if courts were able to carve-out exceptions through piecemeal litigation for "discrete and well-defined instances," women whose circumstances have not been anticipated by prior litigation could well be left unprotected. In treating those women, physicians would risk criminal prosecution, conviction, and imprisonment if they exercise their best judgment as to the safest medical procedure for their patients. The Court is thus gravely mistaken to conclude that narrow as-applied challenges are "the proper manner to protect the health of the woman."

## IV

As the Court wrote in *Casey*, "overruling *Roe*'s central holding would not only reach an unjustifiable result under principles of *stare decisis*, but would seriously weaken the Court's capacity to exercise the judicial power and to function as the Supreme Court of a Nation dedicated to the rule of law." "[T]he very concept of the rule of law underlying our own Constitution requires such continuity over time that a respect for precedent is, by definition, indispensable."

Though today's opinion does not go so far as to discard *Roe* or *Casey*, the Court, differently composed than it was when we last considered a restrictive abortion regulation, is hardly faithful to our earlier invocations of "the rule of law" and the "principles of *stare decisis*." Congress imposed a ban despite our clear prior holdings that the State cannot proscribe an abortion procedure when its use is necessary to protect a woman's health. Although Congress' findings could not withstand the crucible of trial, the Court defers to the legislative override of our Constitution-based rulings. A decision so at odds with our jurisprudence should not have staying power.

In sum, the notion that the Partial-Birth Abortion Ban Act furthers any legitimate governmental interest is, quite simply, irrational. The Court's defense of the statute provides no saving explanation. In candor, the Act, and the Court's defense of it, cannot be understood as anything other than an effort to chip away at a right declared again and again by this Court—and with increasing comprehension of its centrality to women's lives. When "a statute burdens constitutional rights and all that can be said on its behalf is that it is the vehicle that legislators have chosen for expressing their hostility to those rights, the burden is undue."

———

For the reasons stated, I dissent from the Court's disposition and would affirm the judgments before us for review.

# Dissenting Opinion in *Burwell v. Hobby Lobby Stores, Inc.* (2014)

*Passed in 2010, the Affordable Care Act was a sweeping change to the American health care system. Among its provisions was a mandate that companies with more than fifty employees provide affordable health coverage to all their employees, including access to contraception, or else pay a fee. Hobby Lobby, an arts and crafts store, is a "closely-held corporation" owned by the Green family, a group of devout evangelical Christians. The Greens protested the law, arguing that forcing them to provide some forms of contraceptive coverage violated their religious beliefs, and that Hobby Lobby warranted an exemption under the Religious Freedom Restoration Act. In* Burwell v. Hobby Lobby Stores, Inc., *a majority of the Court agreed, ruling that the RFRA applied to closely held corporations, essentially granting those businesses the same religious freedom rights as persons; thus, Hobby Lobby did not have to comply with the contraceptive mandate, given that the government could have accomplished its health care objective in a less restrictive way.*

*In the following dissent, Justice Ginsburg disagrees, writing that RFRA should not be extended to apply to*

> corporations, and that doing so allows corporations to
> impose their religious beliefs on employees. She adds that
> even if RFRA did provide protection here for the
> Greens, the government has a compelling interest in
> protecting women's health through the contraceptive
> mandate that outweighs the Greens' claim.

In a decision of startling breadth, the Court holds that
commercial enterprises, including corporations, along with
partnerships and sole proprietorships, can opt out of any law
(saving only tax laws) they judge incompatible with their sincerely held religious beliefs. Compelling governmental interests in uniform compliance with the law, and disadvantages
that religion-based opt-outs impose on others, hold no sway,
the Court decides, at least when there is a "less restrictive alternative." And such an alternative, the Court suggests, there
always will be whenever, in lieu of tolling an enterprise
claiming a religion-based exemption, the government, i.e.,
the general public, can pick up the tab.

The Court does not pretend that the First Amendment's
Free Exercise Clause demands religion-based accommodations
so extreme, for our decisions leave no doubt on that score. Instead, the Court holds that Congress, in the Religious Freedom Restoration Act of 1993, dictated the extraordinary
religion-based exemptions today's decision endorses. In the
Court's view, RFRA demands accommodation of a for-profit
corporation's religious beliefs no matter the impact that accommodation may have on third parties who do not share the
corporation owners' religious faith—in these cases, thousands
of women employed by Hobby Lobby and Conestoga or dependents of persons those corporations employ. Persuaded

that Congress enacted RFRA to serve a far less radical purpose, and mindful of the havoc the Court's judgment can introduce, I dissent.

# I

"The ability of women to participate equally in the economic and social life of the Nation has been facilitated by their ability to control their reproductive lives." Congress acted on that understanding when, as part of a nationwide insurance program intended to be comprehensive, it called for coverage of preventive care responsive to women's needs. . . .

## A

The Affordable Care Act, in its initial form, specified three categories of preventive care that health plans must cover at no added cost to the plan participant or beneficiary. . . . The scheme had a large gap, however; it left out preventive services that "many women's health advocates and medical professionals believe are critically important." To correct this oversight, Senator Barbara Mikulski introduced the Women's Health Amendment, which added to the ACA's minimum coverage requirements a new category of preventive services specific to women's health. . . .

As altered by the Women's Health Amendment's passage, the ACA requires new insurance plans to include coverage without cost sharing of "such additional preventive care and screenings . . . as provided for in comprehensive guidelines supported by the Health Resources and Services Administration," a unit of HHS. . . .

... [T]he HRSA adopted guidelines recommending coverage of "[a]ll [FDA-] approved contraceptive methods, sterilization procedures, and patient education and counseling for all women with reproductive capacity." Thereafter, HHS, the Department of Labor, and the Department of Treasury promulgated regulations requiring group health plans to include coverage of the contraceptive services recommended in the HRSA guidelines, subject to certain exceptions. This opinion refers to these regulations as the contraceptive coverage requirement. . . .

# II

Any First Amendment Free Exercise Clause claim Hobby Lobby or Conestoga might assert is foreclosed by this Court's decision in *Employment Div., Dept. of Human Resources of Ore.* v. *Smith.* . . . The First Amendment is not offended, *Smith* held, when "prohibiting the exercise of religion . . . is not the object of [governmental regulation] but merely the incidental effect of a generally applicable and otherwise valid provision." The ACA's contraceptive coverage requirement applies generally, it is "otherwise valid," it trains on women's well being, not on the exercise of religion, and any effect it has on such exercise is incidental. . . .

The exemption sought by Hobby Lobby and Conestoga would override significant interests of the corporations' employees and covered dependents. It would deny legions of women who do not hold their employers' beliefs access to contraceptive coverage that the ACA would otherwise secure. . . .

# III

## A

Lacking a tenable claim under the Free Exercise Clause, Hobby Lobby and Conestoga rely on RFRA, a statute instructing that "[g]overnment shall not substantially burden a person's exercise of religion even if the burden results from a rule of general applicability" unless the government shows that application of the burden is "the least restrictive means" to further a "compelling governmental interest. . . ."

The legislative history is correspondingly emphatic on RFRA's aim. . . . [T]he Act reinstates the law as it was prior to *Smith*, without "creat[ing] . . . new rights for any religious practice or for any potential litigant." . . .

## C

With RFRA's restorative purpose in mind, I turn to the Act's application to the instant lawsuits. That task, in view of the positions taken by the Court, requires consideration of several questions, each potentially dispositive of Hobby Lobby's and Conestoga's claims: Do for-profit corporations rank among "person[s]" who "exercise . . . religion"? Assuming that they do, does the contraceptive coverage requirement "substantially burden" their religious exercise? If so, is the requirement "in furtherance of a compelling government interest"? And last, does the requirement represent the least restrictive means for furthering that interest?

Misguided by its errant premise that RFRA moved beyond

the pre-*Smith* case law, the Court falters at each step of its analysis. . . .

1

Until this litigation, no decision of this Court recognized a for-profit corporation's qualification for a religious exemption from a generally applicable law, whether under the Free Exercise Clause or RFRA. The absence of such precedent is just what one would expect, for the exercise of religion is characteristic of natural persons, not artificial legal entities. As Chief Justice Marshall observed nearly two centuries ago, a corporation is "an artificial being, invisible, intangible, and existing only in contemplation of law."

The First Amendment's free exercise protections, the Court has indeed recognized, shelter churches and other nonprofit religion-based organizations. . . . [U]ntil today, religious exemptions had never been extended to any entity operating in "the commercial, profit-making world."

The reason why is hardly obscure. Religious organizations exist to foster the interests of persons subscribing to the same religious faith. Not so of for-profit corporations. Workers who sustain the operations of those corporations commonly are not drawn from one religious community. Indeed, by law, no religion-based criterion can restrict the work force of for-profit corporations. The distinction between a community made up of believers in the same religion and one embracing persons of diverse beliefs, clear as it is, constantly escapes the Court's attention. One can only wonder why the Court shuts this key difference from sight.

Reading RFRA, as the Court does, to require extension of religion-based exemptions to for-profit corporations surely is not grounded in the pre-*Smith* precedent Congress sought to preserve. Had Congress intended RFRA to initiate a change so huge, a clarion statement to that effect likely would have been made in the legislation. . . . The text of RFRA makes no such statement and the legislative history does not so much as mention for-profit corporations. . . .

The Court's determination that RFRA extends to for-profit corporations is bound to have untoward effects. Although the Court attempts to cabin its language to closely held corporations, its logic extends to corporations of any size, public or private. Little doubt that RFRA claims will proliferate, for the Court's expansive notion of corporate personhood—combined with its other errors in construing RFRA—invites for-profit entities to seek religion-based exemptions from regulations they deem offensive to their faith.

2

Even if Hobby Lobby and Conestoga were deemed RFRA "person[s]," to gain an exemption, they must demonstrate that the contraceptive coverage requirement "substantially burden[s] [their] exercise of religion." . . .

The Court barely pauses to inquire whether any burden imposed by the contraceptive coverage requirement is substantial. . . . I agree with the Court that the Green and Hahn families' religious convictions regarding contraception are sincerely held. . . . But those beliefs, however deeply held, do not suffice to sustain a RFRA claim. RFRA, properly understood, distinguishes between "factual allegations that [plaintiffs'] beliefs are sincere and of a religious nature," which a court must accept as true, and the "legal conclusion . . . that [plaintiffs'] religious exercise is substantially burdened," an inquiry the court must undertake.

. . . [T]oday's decision elides entirely the distinction between the sincerity of a challenger's religious belief and the substantiality of the burden placed on the challenger.

Undertaking the inquiry that the Court forgoes, I would conclude that the connection between the families' religious objections and the contraceptive coverage requirement is too attenuated to rank as substantial. The requirement carries no command that Hobby Lobby or Conestoga purchase or provide the contraceptives they find objectionable. Instead, it calls on the companies covered by the requirement to direct money into undifferentiated funds that finance a wide variety of benefits under comprehensive health plans. Those plans, in order to comply with the ACA, must offer contraceptive coverage without cost sharing, just as they must cover an array of other preventive services.

Importantly, the decisions whether to claim benefits under the plans are made not by Hobby Lobby or Conestoga, but by the covered employees and dependents, in consultation with their health care providers. Should an employee of Hobby Lobby or Conestoga share the religious beliefs of the Greens and Hahns, she is of course under no compulsion to use the contraceptives in question. . . . Any decision to use contraceptives made by a woman covered under Hobby Lobby's or Conestoga's plan will not be propelled by the Government, it will be the woman's autonomous choice, informed by the physician she consults.

3

Even if one were to conclude that Hobby Lobby and Conestoga meet the substantial burden requirement, the Government has shown that the contraceptive coverage for which the ACA provides furthers compelling interests in public health and women's well-being. Those interests are concrete, specific, and demonstrated by a wealth of empirical evidence. To recapitulate, the mandated contraception coverage enables women to avoid the health problems unintended pregnancies may visit on them and their children. The coverage helps safeguard the health of women for whom pregnancy may be hazardous, even life threatening. And the mandate secures benefits wholly unrelated to pregnancy, preventing certain cancers, menstrual disorders, and pelvic pain. . . .

The Court ultimately acknowledges a critical point: RFRA's application "must take adequate account of the burdens a requested accommodation may impose on non-beneficiaries." No tradition, and no prior decision under RFRA, allows a religion-based exemption when the accommodation would be harmful to others—here, the very persons the contraceptive coverage requirement was designed to protect.

4

After assuming the existence of compelling government interests, the Court holds that the contraceptive coverage requirement fails to satisfy RFRA's least restrictive means test. But the Government has shown that there is no less restrictive, equally effective means that would both (1) satisfy the challengers' religious objections to providing insurance coverage for certain contraceptives (which they believe cause abortions); and (2) carry out the objective of the ACA's contraceptive coverage requirement, to ensure that women employees receive, at no cost to them, the preventive care needed to safeguard their health and well being. A "least restrictive means" cannot require employees to relinquish benefits accorded them by federal law in order to ensure that their commercial employers can adhere unreservedly to their religious tenets.

As the Court made clear in *Cutter*, the government's license to grant religion-based exemptions from generally applicable laws is constrained by the Establishment Clause. . . . Consequently, one person's right to free exercise must be kept in harmony with the rights of her fellow citizens, and "some religious practices [must] yield to the common good."

Then let the government pay (rather than the employees who do not share their employer's faith), the Court suggests. . . . The ACA, however, requires coverage of preventive services through the existing employer-based system of health insurance "so that [employees] face minimal logistical and administrative obstacles." Impeding women's receipt of benefits "by requiring them to take steps to learn about, and to sign up for, a new [government funded and administered] health benefit" was scarcely what Congress contemplated. . . .

And where is the stopping point to the "let the government pay" alternative? Suppose an employer's sincerely held religious belief is offended by health coverage of vaccines, or paying the minimum wage, or according women equal pay for substantially similar work? Does it rank as a less restrictive alternative to require the government to provide the money or benefit to which the employer has a religion-based objection? . . .

Conestoga suggests that, if its employees had to acquire and pay for the contraceptives (to which the corporation objects) on their own, a tax credit would qualify as a less restrictive alternative. A tax credit, of course, is one variety of "let the government pay." In addition to departing from the existing employer-based system of health insurance, Conestoga's alternative would require a woman to reach into her own pocket in the first instance, and it would do nothing for the woman too poor to be aided by a tax credit.

In sum, in view of what Congress sought to accomplish, i.e., comprehensive preventive care for women furnished through employer-based health plans, none of the proffered alternatives would satisfactorily serve the compelling interests to which Congress responded.

# IV

Among the pathmarking pre-*Smith* decisions RFRA preserved is *United States* v. *Lee* (1982). Lee, a sole proprietor engaged in farming and carpentry, was a member of the Old Order Amish. He sincerely believed that withholding Social Security taxes from his employees or paying the employer's share of such taxes would violate the Amish faith. This Court held that, although the obligations imposed by the Social Security system conflicted with Lee's religious beliefs, the burden was not unconstitutional. The Government urges that *Lee* should control the challenges brought by Hobby Lobby and Conestoga. In contrast, today's Court dismisses *Lee* as a tax case. Indeed, it was a tax case and the Court in *Lee* homed in on "[t]he difficulty in attempting to accommodate religious beliefs in the area of taxation."

But . . . the Court recognized in *Lee* that allowing a religion-based exemption to a commercial employer would "operat[e] to impose the employer's religious faith on the employees." No doubt the Greens and Hahns and all who share their beliefs may decline to acquire for themselves the contraceptives in question. But that choice may not be imposed on employees who hold other beliefs. . . .

. . . Hobby Lobby and Conestoga surely do not stand alone as commercial enterprises seeking exemptions from generally applicable laws on the basis of their religious beliefs. . . . [H]ow does the Court divine which religious beliefs are worthy of accommodation, and which are not? Isn't the Court disarmed from making such a judgment given its recognition that "courts must not presume to determine . . . the plausibility of a religious claim"?

Would the exemption the Court holds RFRA demands for employers with religiously grounded objections to the use of certain contraceptives extend to employers with religiously grounded objections to blood transfusions (Jehovah's Witnesses); antidepressants (Scientologists); medications derived from pigs, including anesthesia, intravenous fluids, and pills coated with gelatin (certain Muslims, Jews, and Hindus); and vaccinations (Christian Scientists, among others)? According to counsel for Hobby Lobby, "each one of these cases . . . would have to be evaluated on its own . . . apply[ing] the compelling interest-least restrictive alternative test." Not much help there for the lower courts bound by today's decision.

The Court, however, sees nothing to worry about. Today's cases, the Court concludes, are "concerned solely with the contraceptive mandate. . . ." The Court has assumed, for RFRA purposes, that the interest in women's health and well being is compelling and has come up with no means adequate to serve that interest, the one motivating Congress to adopt the Women's Health Amendment.

There is an overriding interest, I believe, in keeping the courts "out of the business of evaluating the relative merits of differing religious claims," or the sincerity with which an asserted religious belief is held. Indeed, approving some religious claims while deeming others unworthy of accommodation could be "perceived as favoring one religion over another," the very "risk the Establishment Clause was designed to preclude." The Court, I fear, has ventured into a minefield by its immoderate reading of RFRA. I would confine religious exemptions under that Act to organizations formed "for a religious purpose," "engage[d] primarily in carrying out that religious purpose," and not "engaged . . . substantially in the exchange of goods or services for money beyond nominal amounts."

———

For the reasons stated, I would reverse the judgment of the Court of Appeals for the Tenth Circuit and affirm the judgment of the Court of Appeals for the Third Circuit.

# Concurring Opinion in
## *Whole Woman's Health*
## *v. Hellerstedt* **(2016)**

*Texas passed a law in 2013 requiring that physicians be affiliated with a nearby hospital in order to perform abortions and that all abortion clinics must meet the state's standards for certain surgical facilities. Some proponents of the law argued its purpose was to ensure that abortions were safely and properly performed. Opponents said the requirements were unjust because they made it harder for women to receive legal abortions. The Supreme Court, in a 5–3 ruling, took the opponents' side, striking down the law as unconstitutional. Justice Breyer wrote that the Texas law put a "substantial obstacle" on women seeking to exercise their constitutionally granted right to an abortion, without actually furthering the state's interest in improving health care. Here, Justice Ginsburg's concurring opinion emphasizes that modern abortion is a highly safe medical practice, and that a law whose clear purpose is to limit abortion cannot stand under* Roe *and* Casey.

The Texas law called H. B. 2 inevitably will reduce the number of clinics and doctors allowed to provide abortion services. Texas argues that H. B. 2's restrictions are constitutional because they protect the health of women who experience complications from abortions. In truth, "complications from an abortion are both rare and rarely dangerous." Many medical procedures, including childbirth, are far more dangerous to patients, yet are not subject to ambulatory-surgical-center or hospital admitting-privileges requirements. . . . Given those realities, it is beyond rational belief that H. B. 2 could genuinely protect the health of women, and certain that the law "would simply make it more difficult for them to obtain abortions." When a State severely limits access to safe and legal procedures, women in desperate circumstances may resort to unlicensed rogue practitioners, *faute de mieux*, at great risk to their health and safety. So long as this Court adheres to *Roe* v. *Wade* (1973), and *Planned Parenthood of Southeastern Pa.* v. *Casey* (1992), Targeted Regulation of Abortion Providers laws like H. B. 2 that "do little or nothing for health, but rather strew impediments to abortion," cannot survive judicial inspection.

# *Part III*

# VOTING
## *and*
# CIVIL RIGHTS

Now, it is true . . . that the immediate implementation in the days of the founding fathers in many respects was limited. "We the people" was not then what it is today. The most eloquent speaker on that subject was Justice Thurgood Marshall, when during the celebration of the bicentennial, when songs of praise to the Constitution were sung, he reminded us that the Constitution's immediate implementation, even its text, had certain limitations, blind spots, blots on our record. But he said that the beauty of this Constitution is that through a combination of interpretation, constitutional amendment, laws passed by Congress, "we the people" has grown ever larger. So now it includes people who were once held in bondage; it includes women, who were left out of the political community at the start.

—RUTH BADER GINSBURG,
SENATE CONFIRMATION HEARING, JULY 20, 1993

# Dissenting Opinion in *Adarand Constructors, Inc. v. Peña* (1995)

*Most federal government contracts at the time of this case included a provision adding a funding incentive for contractors to choose "socially and economically disadvantaged individuals" to work with. The "contractor shall presume that socially and economically disadvantaged individuals include Black Americans, Hispanic Americans, Native Americans, Asian Pacific Americans, and other minorities. . . ." Gonzales Construction Company was then selected for a contract instead of Adarand because of the additional money the contractor received for choosing the minority-led Gonzales. The Supreme Court sided with Adarand's challenge, writing that the race-based classification system could not survive the strict scrutiny it demanded under the Equal Protection Clause; the Court could not assume some contractors were "disadvantaged" based purely on race.*

*Justice Ginsburg dissented, highlighting her view that the Equal Protection Clause was not meant to be blind to race or gender; rather, it demands policies that are meant to advance true equality for groups that have been traditionally marginalized in society.*

For the reasons stated by Justice Souter, and in view of the attention the political branches are currently giving the matter of affirmative action, I see no compelling cause for the intervention the Court has made in this case. I further agree with Justice Stevens that, in this area, large deference is owed by the Judiciary to "Congress' institutional competence and constitutional authority to overcome historic racial subjugation." I write separately to underscore not the differences the several opinions in this case display, but the considerable field of agreement—the common understandings and concerns— revealed in opinions that together speak for a majority of the Court.

# I

The statutes and regulations at issue, as the Court indicates, were adopted by the political branches in response to an "unfortunate reality": "[t]he unhappy persistence of both the practice and the lingering effects of racial discrimination against minority groups in this country." The United States suffers from those lingering effects because, for most of our Nation's history, the idea that "we are just one race" was not embraced. For generations, our lawmakers and judges were unprepared to say that there is in this land no superior race, no race inferior to any other. In *Plessy* v. *Ferguson*, not only did this Court endorse the oppressive practice of race segregation, but even Justice Harlan, the advocate of a "colorblind" Constitution, stated:

> The white race deems itself to be the dominant race in this country. And so it is, in prestige, in achievements, in education, in wealth and in power. So, I doubt not,

it will continue to be for all time, if it remains true to its great heritage and holds fast to the principles of constitutional liberty.

Not until *Loving* v. *Virginia* (1967), which held unconstitutional Virginia's ban on interracial marriages, could one say with security that the Constitution and this Court would abide no measure "designed to maintain White Supremacy."

The divisions in this difficult case should not obscure the Court's recognition of the persistence of racial inequality and a majority's acknowledgement of Congress' authority to act affirmatively, not only to end discrimination, but also to counteract discrimination's lingering effects. Those effects, reflective of a system of racial caste only recently ended, are evident in our workplaces, markets, and neighborhoods. Job applicants with identical resumes, qualifications, and interview styles still experience different receptions, depending on their race. White and African-American consumers still encounter different deals. People of color looking for housing still face discriminatory treatment by landlords, real estate agents, and mortgage lenders. Minority entrepreneurs sometimes fail to gain contracts though they are the low bidders, and they are sometimes refused work even after winning contracts. Bias both conscious and unconscious, reflecting traditional and unexamined habits of thought, keeps up barriers that must come down if equal opportunity and nondiscrimination are ever genuinely to become this country's law and practice.

Given this history and its practical consequences, Congress surely can conclude that a carefully designed affirmative action program may help to realize, finally, the "equal protection of the laws" the Fourteenth Amendment has promised since 1868.

# II

The lead opinion uses one term, "strict scrutiny," to describe the standard of judicial review for all governmental classifications by race. But that opinion's elaboration strongly suggests that the strict standard announced is indeed "fatal" for classifications burdening groups that have suffered discrimination in our society. That seems to me, and, I believe, to the Court, the enduring lesson one should draw from *Korematsu* v. *United States* (1944); for in that case, scrutiny the Court described as "most rigid," nonetheless yielded a pass for an odious, gravely injurious racial classification. A *Korematsu*-type classification, as I read the opinions in this case, will never again survive scrutiny: such a classification, history and precedent instruct, properly ranks as prohibited.

For a classification made to hasten the day when "we are just one race," however, the lead opinion has dispelled the notion that "strict scrutiny" is "'fatal in fact.'" Properly, a majority of the Court calls for review that is searching, in order to ferret out classifications in reality malign, but masquerading as benign. The Court's once lax review of sex-based classifications demonstrates the need for such suspicion. . . . Today's decision thus usefully reiterates that the purpose of strict scrutiny "is precisely to distinguish legitimate from illegitimate uses of race in governmental decision making" "to 'differentiate between' permissible and impermissible governmental use of race" to distinguish "'between a "No Trespassing" sign and a welcome mat.'"

Close review also is in order for this further reason. As Justice Souter points out, and as this very case shows, some members of the historically favored race can be hurt by catch-up mechanisms designed to cope with the lingering effects of entrenched racial subjugation. Court review can ensure that preferences are not so large as to trammel unduly upon the opportunities of others or interfere too harshly with legitimate expectations of persons in once-preferred groups.

———

While I would not disturb the programs challenged in this case, and would leave their improvement to the political branches, I see today's decision as one that allows our precedent to evolve, still to be informed by and responsive to changing conditions.

# Majority Opinion in
# *Olmstead v. L.C.* (1999)

*Justice Ginsburg focused much of her early career on gender equality, but her vision of equality has never been limited to ending only one form of discrimination. Many aspects of public life had long been inaccessible to people with disabilities. So in 1990, Congress passed the Americans with Disabilities Act, a sweeping statute that banned discrimination based on disability in employment, transportation, access to state services, and other areas. Yet full inclusion was not realized with just the stroke of a pen. In this case, two women with psychological disorders were determined by professionals to be stable enough for community-based support. Both, however, remained institutionalized, against their wishes. Justice Ginsburg's majority opinion ruled that under the right circumstances, the ADA requires disabled patients to have the option for community-based care; a patient's choice cannot be between institutionalization and nothing. While the case was decided on the statutory grounds of the ADA (and not the Equal Protection Clause), it demonstrates Justice Ginsburg's concern with making equality central to American law.*

This case concerns the proper construction of the anti-discrimination provision contained in the public services portion (Title II) of the Americans with Disabilities Act of 1990. Specifically, we confront the question whether the proscription of discrimination may require placement of persons with mental disabilities in community settings rather than in institutions. The answer, we hold, is a qualified yes. Such action is in order when the State's treatment professionals have determined that community placement is appropriate, the transfer from institutional care to a less restrictive setting is not opposed by the affected individual, and the placement can be reasonably accommodated, taking into account the resources available to the State and the needs of others with mental disabilities. In so ruling, we affirm the decision of the Eleventh Circuit in substantial part. We remand the case, however, for further consideration of the appropriate relief, given the range of facilities the State maintains for the care and treatment of persons with diverse mental disabilities, and its obligation to administer services with an even hand.

## I . . .

In the opening provisions of the ADA, Congress stated findings applicable to the statute in all its parts. Most relevant to this case, Congress determined that

"(2) historically, society has tended to isolate and segregate individuals with disabilities, and, despite some improvements, such forms of discrimination against individuals with disabilities continue to be a serious and pervasive social problem;

"(3) discrimination against individuals with disabilities persists in such critical areas as . . . institutionalization . . . ;

"(5) individuals with disabilities continually encounter various forms of discrimination, including outright intentional exclusion, . . . failure to make modifications to existing facilities and practices, . . . [and] segregation. . . ."

Congress then set forth prohibitions against discrimination in employment, public services furnished by governmental entities, and public accommodations provided by private entities. The statute as a whole is intended "to provide a clear and comprehensive national mandate for the elimination of discrimination against individuals with disabilities."

This case concerns Title II, the public services portion of the ADA. The provision of Title II centrally at issue reads:

"Subject to the provisions of this subchapter, no qualified individual with a disability shall, by reason of such disability, be excluded from participation in or be denied the benefits of the services, programs, or activities of a public entity, or be subjected to discrimination by any such entity."

Title [II] . . . defines "qualified individual with a disability" as "an individual with a disability who, with or without reasonable modifications to rules, policies, or practices, the removal of architectural, communication, or transportation barriers, or the provision of auxiliary aids and services, meets the essential eligibility requirements for the receipt of services or the participation in programs or activities provided by a public entity." On redress for violations of discrimination prohibition, Congress referred to remedies available under the Rehabilitation Act of 1973.

Congress instructed the Attorney General to issue regulations implementing provisions of Title II, including discrimination proscription. . . .

As Congress instructed, the Attorney General issued Title II regulations, including one . . . called the "integration regulation," it reads:

> "A public entity shall administer services, programs, and activities in the most integrated setting appropriate to the needs of qualified individuals with disabilities."

The preamble to the Attorney General's Title II regulations defines "the most integrated setting appropriate to the needs of qualified individuals with disabilities" to mean "a setting that enables individuals with disabilities to interact with non-disabled persons to the fullest extent possible." Another regulation requires public entities to "make reasonable modifications" to avoid "discrimination on the basis of disability," unless those modifications would entail a "fundamenta[l] alter[ation]"; called here the "reasonable-modifications regulation," it provides:

> "A public entity shall make reasonable modifications in policies, practices, or procedures when the modifications are necessary to avoid discrimination on the basis of disability, unless the public entity can demonstrate

that making the modifications would fundamentally
alter the nature of the service, program, or activity."

We recite these regulations with the caveat that we do not
here determine their validity. While the parties differ on the
proper construction and enforcement of the regulations, we
do not understand petitioners to challenge the regulatory
formulations themselves as outside the congressional autho-
rization.

# II

With the key legislative provisions in full view, we summarize the facts underlying this dispute. Respondents L. C. and
E. W. are mentally retarded women; L. C. has also been diagnosed with schizophrenia, and E. W., with a personality
disorder. Both women have a history of treatment in institutional settings. In May 1992, L. C. was voluntarily admitted
to Georgia Regional Hospital at Atlanta (GRH), where she
was confined for treatment in a psychiatric unit. By May
1993, her psychiatric condition had stabilized, and L. C.'s
treatment team at GRH agreed that her needs could be met
appropriately in one of the community-based programs the
State supported. Despite this evaluation, L. C. remained institutionalized until February 1996, when the State placed
her in a community-based treatment program.

E. W. was voluntarily admitted to GRH in February
1995; like L. C., E. W. was confined for treatment in a
psychiatric unit. In March 1995, GRH sought to discharge
E. W. to a homeless shelter, but abandoned that plan after
her attorney filed an administrative complaint. By 1996,

E. W. 's treating psychiatrist concluded that she could be treated appropriately in a community-based setting. She nonetheless remained institutionalized until a few months after the District Court issued its judgment in this case in 1997.

In May 1995, when she was still institutionalized at GRH, L. C. filed suit in the United States District Court for the Northern District of Georgia, challenging her continued confinement in a segregated environment. . . . L. C. alleged that the State's failure to place her in a community-based program, once her treating professionals determined that such placement was appropriate, violated Title II of the ADA. L. C. 's pleading requested, among other things, that the State place her in a community care residential program, and that she receive treatment with the ultimate goal of integrating her into the mainstream of society. E. W. intervened in the action, stating an identical claim.

The District Court granted partial summary judgment in favor of L. C. and E. W. The court held that the State's failure to place L. C. and E. W. in an appropriate community-based treatment program violated Title II of the ADA. . . .

. . . Rejecting the State's "fundamental alteration" defense, the court observed that existing state programs provided community-based treatment of the kind for which L. C. and E. W. qualified, and that the State could "provide services to plaintiffs in the community at considerably less cost than is required to maintain them in an institution."

The Court of Appeals for the Eleventh Circuit affirmed the judgment of the District Court, but remanded for reassessment of the State's cost-based defense. . . .

We granted certiorari in view of the importance of the question presented to the States and affected individuals.

# III

Endeavoring to carry out Congress' instruction to issue regulations implementing Title II, the Attorney General, in the
integration and reasonable-modifications regulations, made
two key determinations. The first concerned the scope of the
ADA's discrimination proscription; the second concerned
the obligation of the States to counter discrimination. As to
the first, the Attorney General concluded that unjustified
placement or retention of persons in institutions, severely
limiting their exposure to the outside community, constitutes
a form of discrimination based on disability prohibited by
Title II. Regarding the States' obligation to avoid unjustified
isolation of individuals with disabilities, the Attorney General provided that States could resist modifications that
"would fundamentally alter the nature of the service, program, or activity."

The Court of Appeals essentially upheld the Attorney
General's construction of the ADA. . . .

We affirm the Court of Appeals' decision in substantial
part. Unjustified isolation, we hold, is properly regarded as
discrimination based on disability. But we recognize, as well,
the States' need to maintain a range of facilities for the care
and treatment of persons with diverse mental disabilities, and
the States' obligation to administer services with an even
hand. Accordingly, we further hold that the Court of Appeals' remand instruction was unduly restrictive. In evaluating a State's fundamental-alteration defense, the District
Court must consider, in view of the resources available to the
State, not only the cost of providing community-based care
to the litigants, but also the range of services the State pro-

vides others with mental disabilities, and the State's obligation to mete out those services equitably.

### A

We examine first whether, as the Eleventh Circuit held, undue institutionalization qualifies as discrimination "by reason of . . . disability." The Department of Justice has consistently advocated that it does. Because the Department is the agency directed by Congress to issue regulations implementing Title II, its views warrant respect. . . .

The State argues that L. C. and E. W. encountered no discrimination "by reason of" their disabilities because they were not denied community placement on account of those disabilities. Nor were they subjected to "discrimination," the State contends, because "'discrimination' necessarily requires uneven treatment of similarly situated individuals," and L. C. and E. W. had identified no comparison class, i.e., no similarly situated individuals given preferential treatment. We are satisfied that Congress had a more comprehensive view of the concept of discrimination advanced in the ADA.

. . . Ultimately, in the ADA, enacted in 1990, Congress not only required all public entities to refrain from discrimination; additionally, in findings applicable to the entire statute, Congress explicitly identified unjustified "segregation" of persons with disabilities as a "for[m] of discrimination." . . .

Recognition that unjustified institutional isolation of persons with disabilities is a form of discrimination reflects two evident judgments. First, institutional placement of persons who can handle and benefit from community settings perpetuates unwarranted assumptions that persons so isolated are incapable or unworthy of participating in community life. . . . Second, confinement in an institution severely diminishes the everyday life activities of individuals, including family relations, social contacts, work options, economic independence, educational advancement, and cultural enrichment. Dissimilar treatment correspondingly exists in this key respect: In order to receive needed medical services, persons with mental disabilities must, because of those disabilities, relinquish participation in community life they could enjoy given reasonable accommodations, while persons without mental disabilities can receive the medical services they need without similar sacrifice. . . .

We emphasize that nothing in the ADA or its implementing regulations condones termination of institutional settings for persons unable to handle or benefit from community settings. Title II provides only that "qualified individual[s] with a disability" may not "be subjected to discrimination." "Qualified individuals," the ADA further explains, are persons with disabilities who, "with or without reasonable modifications to rules, policies, or practices, . . . mee[t] the essential eligibility requirements for the receipt of services or the participation in programs or activities provided by a public entity."

Consistent with these provisions, the State generally may rely on the reasonable assessments of its own professionals in determining whether an individual "meets the essential eligibility requirements" for habilitation in a community-based program. Absent such qualification, it would be inappropriate to remove a patient from the more restrictive setting. . . . In this case, however, there is no genuine dispute concerning the status of L. C. and E. W. as individuals "qualified" for noninstitutional care: The State's own professionals determined that community-based treatment would be appropriate for L. C. and E. W., and neither woman opposed such treatment.

## B

The State's responsibility, once it provides community-based treatment to qualified persons with disabilities, is not boundless. The reasonable-modifications regulation speaks of "reasonable modifications" to avoid discrimination, and allows States to resist modifications that entail a "fundamenta[l] alter[ation]" of the States' services and programs. The Court of Appeals construed this regulation to permit a cost-based defense "only in the most limited of circumstances," and remanded to the District Court to consider, among other things, "whether the additional expenditures necessary to treat L. C. and E. W. in community-based care would be unreasonable given the demands of the State's mental health budget."

The Court of Appeals' construction of the reasonable-modifications regulation is unacceptable for it would leave the State virtually defenseless once it is shown that the plaintiff is qualified for the service or program she seeks. If the expense entailed in placing one or two people in a community-based treatment program is properly measured for reasonableness against the State's entire mental health budget, it is unlikely that a State, relying on the fundamental-alteration defense, could ever prevail. . . . Sensibly construed, the fundamental-alteration component of the reasonable-modifications regulation would allow the State to show that, in the allocation of available resources, immediate relief for the plaintiffs would be inequitable, given the responsibility the State has undertaken for the care and treatment of a large and diverse population of persons with mental disabilities. . . .

As already observed, the ADA is not reasonably read to

impel States to phase out institutions, placing patients in need of close care at risk. . . . Nor is it the ADA's mission to drive States to move institutionalized patients into an inappropriate setting, such as a homeless shelter, a placement the State proposed, then retracted, for E. W. Some individuals, like L. C. and E. W. in prior years, may need institutional care from time to time "to stabilize acute psychiatric symptoms." . . . For other individuals, no placement outside the institution may ever be appropriate.

To maintain a range of facilities and to administer services with an even hand, the State must have more leeway than the courts below understood the fundamental-alteration defense to allow. If, for example, the State were to demonstrate that it had a comprehensive, effectively working plan for placing qualified persons with mental disabilities in less restrictive settings, and a waiting list that moved at a reasonable pace not controlled by the State's endeavors to keep its institutions fully populated, the reasonable-modifications standard would be met. . . . In such circumstances, a court would have no warrant effectively to order displacement of persons at the top of the community-based treatment waiting list by individuals lower down who commenced civil actions.

━━

For the reasons stated, we conclude that, under Title II of the ADA, States are required to provide community-based treatment for persons with mental disabilities when the State's treatment professionals determine that such placement is appropriate, the affected persons do not oppose such treatment, and the placement can be reasonably accommodated, taking into account the resources available to the State and the needs of others with mental disabilities. The judgment of the Eleventh Circuit is therefore affirmed in part and vacated in part, and the case is remanded for further proceedings consistent with this opinion.

*It is so ordered.*

# Dissenting Opinion in
## *Bush v. Gore* (2000)

*Democrat Al Gore and Republican George W. Bush faced off in the 2000 presidential election. A historically close race, the final Electoral College tally came down to a disputed vote total in Florida. A fight over the recount ultimately reached the Supreme Court. The Court ruled that no recount consistent with constitutional principles could finish in the time remaining before the election results needed to be certified. The Court also noted that without a uniform standard to judge recount votes, not everyone's vote would count the same, violating equal protection. The ruling effectively awarded Florida, and with it the presidency, to Bush. Justice Ginsburg's dissent put her in an unusual position: arguing against an equal protection claim. In the dissent, she argues that the Court should have respected the principles of federalism and abided by the ruling of the Florida Supreme Court, letting the recount go forward unobstructed.*

The Chief Justice acknowledges that provisions of Florida's Election Code "may well admit of more than one interpretation." But instead of respecting the state high court's province to say what the State's Election Code means, the Chief Justice maintains that Florida's Supreme Court has veered so far from the ordinary practice of judicial review that what it did cannot properly be called judging. My colleagues have offered a reasonable construction of Florida's law. Their construction coincides with the view of one of Florida's seven Supreme Court justices. I might join the Chief Justice were it my commission to interpret Florida law. But disagreement with the Florida court's interpretation of its own State's law does not warrant the conclusion that the justices of that court have legislated. There is no cause here to believe that the members of Florida's high court have done less than "their mortal best to discharge their oath of office," and no cause to upset their reasoned interpretation of Florida law.

This Court more than occasionally affirms statutory, and even constitutional, interpretations with which it disagrees. For example, when reviewing challenges to administrative agencies' interpretations of laws they implement, we defer to the agencies unless their interpretation violates "the unambiguously expressed intent of Congress." We do so in the face of the declaration in Article I of the United States Constitution that "All legislative Powers herein granted shall be vested in a Congress of the United States." Surely the Constitution does not call upon us to pay more respect to a federal administrative agency's construction of federal law than to a state high court's interpretation of its own state's law. And not uncommonly, we let stand state-court interpretations of federal law with which we might disagree. . . .

No doubt there are cases in which the proper application of federal law may hinge on interpretations of state law.

Unavoidably, this Court must sometimes examine state law in order to protect federal rights. But we have dealt with such cases ever mindful of the full measure of respect we owe to interpretations of state law by a State's highest court. . . .

In deferring to state courts on matters of state law, we appropriately recognize that this Court acts as an "'outside[r]' lacking the common exposure to local law which comes from sitting in the jurisdiction." That recognition has sometimes prompted us to resolve doubts about the meaning of state law by certifying issues to a State's highest court, even when federal rights are at stake. . . . Notwithstanding our authority to decide issues of state law underlying federal claims, we have used the certification devise to afford state high courts an opportunity to inform us on matters of their own State's law because such restraint "helps build a cooperative judicial federalism."

Just last Term, in *Fiore* v. *White* (1999), we took advantage of Pennsylvania's certification procedure. In that case, a state prisoner brought a federal habeas action claiming that the State had failed to prove an essential element of his charged offense in violation of the Due Process Clause. Instead of resolving the state-law question on which the federal claim depended, we certified the question to the Pennsylvania Supreme Court for that court to "help determine the proper state-law predicate for our determination of the federal constitutional questions raised." The Chief Justice's willingness to *reverse* the Florida Supreme Court's interpretation of Florida law in this case is at least in tension with our reluctance in *Fiore* even to interpret Pennsylvania law before seeking instruction from the Pennsylvania Supreme Court. I would have thought the "cautious approach" we counsel when federal courts address matters of state law and our commitment to "build[ing] cooperative judicial federalism," demanded greater restraint.

Rarely has this Court rejected outright an interpretation of state law by a state high court. *Fairfax's Devisee* v. *Hunter's Lessee* (1813), *NAACP* v. *Alabama ex rel. Patterson* (1958), and *Bouie* v. *City of Columbia* (1964), cited by the Chief Justice, are three such rare instances. But those cases are embedded in historical contexts hardly comparable to the situation here. *Fairfax's Devisee*, which held that the Virginia Court of Appeals had misconstrued its own forfeiture laws to deprive a British subject of lands secured to him by federal treaties, occurred amidst vociferous States' rights attacks on the Marshall Court. The Virginia court refused to obey this Court's *Fairfax's Devisee* mandate to enter judgment for the British subject's successor in interest. That refusal led to the Court's pathmarking decision in *Martin* v. *Hunter's Lessee* (1816). *Patterson*, a case decided three months after *Cooper* v. *Aaron*, 358 U.S. 1 (1958), in the face of Southern resistance to the civil rights movement, held that the Alabama Supreme Court had irregularly applied its own procedural rules to deny review of a contempt order against the NAACP arising from its refusal to disclose membership lists. We said that "our jurisdiction is not defeated if the nonfederal ground relied on by the state court is without any fair or substantial support." *Bouie*, stemming from a lunch counter "sit-in" at the height of the civil rights movement, held that the South Carolina Supreme Court's construction of its trespass laws—criminalizing conduct not covered by the text of an otherwise clear statute— was "unforeseeable" and thus violated due process when applied retroactively to the petitioners.

The Chief Justice's casual citation of these cases might lead one to believe they are part of a larger collection of cases in which we said that the Constitution impelled us to train a skeptical eye on a state court's portrayal of state law. But one would be hard pressed, I think, to find additional cases that fit the mold. As Justice Breyer convincingly explains, this case involves nothing close to the kind of recalcitrance by a state high court that warrants extraordinary action by this Court. The Florida Supreme Court concluded that counting every legal vote was the overriding concern of the Florida Legislature when it enacted the State's Election Code. The court surely should not be bracketed with state high courts of the Jim Crow South.

The Chief Justice says that Article II, by providing that state legislatures shall direct the manner of appointing electors, authorizes federal superintendence over the relationship between state courts and state legislatures, and licenses a departure from the usual deference we give to state court interpretations of state law. . . . The Framers of our Constitution, however, understood that in a republican government, the judiciary would construe the legislature's enactments. In light of the constitutional guarantee to States of a "Republican Form of Government," Article II can hardly be read to invite this Court to disrupt a State's republican regime. Yet the Chief Justice today would reach out to do just that. By holding that Article II requires our revision of a state court's construction of state laws in order to protect one organ of the State from another, the Chief Justice contradicts the basic principle that a State may organize itself as it sees fit. . . . Article II does not call for the scrutiny undertaken by this Court.

The extraordinary setting of this case has obscured the ordinary principle that dictates its proper resolution: Federal courts defer to state high courts' interpretations of their state's own law. This principle reflects the core of federalism, on which all agree. "The Framers split the atom of sovereignty. It was the genius of their idea that our citizens would have two political capacities, one state and one federal, each protected from incursion by the other." . . . Were the other members of this Court as mindful as they generally are of our system of dual sovereignty, they would affirm the judgment of the Florida Supreme Court.

## II

I agree with Justice Stevens that petitioners have not presented a substantial equal protection claim. Ideally, perfection would be the appropriate standard for judging the recount. But we live in an imperfect world, one in which thousands of votes have not been counted. I cannot agree that the recount adopted by the Florida court, flawed as it may be, would yield a result any less fair or precise than the certification that preceded that recount.

Even if there were an equal protection violation, I would agree with Justice Stevens, Justice Souter, and Justice Breyer that the Court's concern about the December date is misplaced. Time is short in part because of the Court's entry of a stay on December 9, several hours after an able circuit judge in Leon County had begun to superintend the recount process. More fundamentally, the Court's reluctance to let the recount go forward—despite its suggestion that "[t]he search for intent can be confined by specific rules designed to ensure uniform treatment"—ultimately turns on its own judgment about the practical realities of implementing a recount, not the judgment of those much closer to the process.

Equally important, as Justice Breyer explains, the December 12 date for bringing Florida's electoral votes into 3 U. S. C. §5's safe harbor lacks the significance the Court assigns it. Were that date to pass, Florida would still be entitled to deliver electoral votes Congress must count unless both Houses find that the votes "ha[d] not been . . . regularly given." The statute identifies other significant dates. . . . December 18 as the date electors "shall meet and give their votes" . . . "the fourth Wednesday in December"—this year, December 27—as the date on which Congress, if it has not received a State's electoral votes, shall request the state secretary of state to send a certified return immediately. But none of these dates has ultimate significance in light of Congress' detailed provisions for determining, on "the sixth day of January," the validity of electoral votes.

The Court assumes that time will not permit "orderly judicial review of any disputed matters that might arise." But no one has doubted the good faith and diligence with which Florida election officials, attorneys for all sides of this controversy, and the courts of law have performed their duties. Notably, the Florida Supreme Court has produced two substantial opinions within 29 hours of oral argument. In sum, the Court's conclusion that a constitutionally adequate recount is impractical is a prophecy the Court's own judgment will not allow to be tested. Such an untested prophecy should not decide the Presidency of the United States.

I dissent.

# Dissenting Opinion in
## *Ricci v. DeStefano* (2009)

*Justice Ginsburg's dissent against color-blindness in* Adarand *could not keep affirmative action from remaining a thorny issue for courts in the early 2000s. This case dealt with a lawsuit filed by a group of mostly white firefighters in New Haven, Connecticut, who sued their fire department because their promotions had not been certified in an effort to ensure more nonwhite candidates in leadership positions. Justice Anthony Kennedy's majority opinion invalidated New Haven's failure to certify the tests, arguing that a city cannot draw race-based distinctions unless it was clear the city would face "disparate impact liability" for failing to do so. Justice Ginsburg dissented, arguing that the Court was wrongly restricting New Haven from rectifying discriminatory practices that had adversely harmed nonwhite firefighters and that the city was right to seek to avoid liability for discriminatory practices.*

In assessing claims of race discrimination, "[c]ontext matters." In 1972, Congress extended Title VII of the Civil Rights Act of 1964 to cover public employment. At that time, municipal fire departments across the country, including New Haven's, pervasively discriminated against minorities. The extension of Title VII to cover jobs in firefighting effected no overnight change. It took decades of persistent effort, advanced by Title VII litigation, to open firefighting posts to members of racial minorities.

The white firefighters who scored high on New Haven's promotional exams understandably attract this Court's sympathy. But they had no vested right to promotion. Nor have other persons received promotions in preference to them. New Haven maintains that it refused to certify the test results because it believed, for good cause, that it would be vulnerable to a Title VII disparate-impact suit if it relied on those results. The Court today holds that New Haven has not demonstrated "a strong basis in evidence" for its plea. In so holding, the Court pretends that "[t]he City rejected the test results solely because the higher scoring candidates were white." That pretension, essential to the Court's disposition, ignores substantial evidence of multiple flaws in the tests New Haven used. The Court similarly fails to acknowledge the better tests used in other cities, which have yielded less racially skewed outcomes.

By order of this Court, New Haven, a city in which African-Americans and Hispanics account for nearly 60 percent of the population, must today be served—as it was in the days of undisguised discrimination—by a fire department in which members of racial and ethnic minorities are rarely seen in command positions. . . . The Court's order and opinion, I anticipate, will not have staying power.

# I

## A

The Court's recitation of the facts leaves out important parts of the story. Firefighting is a profession in which the legacy of racial discrimination casts an especially long shadow. In extending Title VII to state and local government employers in 1972, Congress took note of a U.S. Commission on Civil Rights (USCCR) report finding racial discrimination in municipal employment even "more pervasive than in the private sector." . . . The USCCR report singled out police and fire departments for having "[b]arriers to equal employment . . . greater . . . than in any other area of State or local government," with African-Americans "hold[ing] almost no positions in the officer ranks."

The city of New Haven (City) was no exception. In the early 1970's, African-Americans and Hispanics composed 30 percent of New Haven's population, but only 3.6 percent of the City's 502 firefighters. The racial disparity in the officer ranks was even more pronounced: "[O]f the 107 officers in the Department only one was black, and he held the lowest rank above private."

Following a lawsuit and settlement agreement, the City initiated efforts to increase minority representation in the New Haven Fire Department. Those litigation-induced efforts produced some positive change. Among entry-level firefighters, minorities are still underrepresented, but not starkly so. As of 2003, African-Americans and Hispanics constituted 30 percent and 16 percent of the City's firefighters, respectively. In supervisory positions, however, significant disparities remain. Overall, the senior officer ranks (captain and higher) are nine percent African-American and nine percent Hispanic. . . . It is against this backdrop of entrenched inequality that the promotion process at issue in this litigation should be assessed.

## B

By order of its charter, New Haven must use competitive examinations to fill vacancies in fire officer and other civil-service positions. . . .

New Haven, the record indicates, did not closely consider what sort of "practical" examination would "fairly measure the relative fitness and capacity of the applicants to discharge the duties" of a fire officer. Instead, the City simply adhered to the testing regime outlined in its two-decades-old contract with the local firefighters' union: a written exam, which would account for 60 percent of an applicant's total score, and an oral exam, which would account for the remaining 40 percent. In soliciting bids from exam development companies, New Haven made clear that it would entertain only "proposals that include a written component that will be weighted at 60%, and an oral component that will be weighted at 40%." . . .

Pursuant to New Haven's specifications, IOS developed and administered the oral and written exams. The results showed significant racial disparities. On the lieutenant exam, the pass rate for African-American candidates was about one-half the rate for Caucasian candidates; the pass rate for Hispanic candidates was even lower. On the captain exam, both African-American and Hispanic candidates passed at about half the rate of their Caucasian counterparts. More striking still, although nearly half of the 77 lieutenant candidates were African-American or Hispanic, none would have been eligible for promotion to the eight positions then vacant. . . . As for the seven then-vacant captain positions, two Hispanic candidates would have been eligible, but no African-Americans. . . .

These stark disparities, the Court acknowledges, sufficed to state a . . . case under Title VII's disparate-impact provision. New Haven thus had cause for concern about the prospect of Title VII litigation and liability. City officials referred the matter to the New Haven Civil Service Board (CSB), the entity responsible for certifying the results of employment exams.

. . . [T]heir principal task was to decide whether they were confident about the reliability of the exams: Had the exams fairly measured the qualities of a successful fire officer despite their disparate results? Might an alternative examination process have identified the most qualified candidates without creating such significant racial imbalances?

Seeking a range of input on these questions, the CSB heard from test takers, the test designer, subject-matter experts, City officials, union leaders, and community members. . . .

A representative of the Northeast Region of the International Association of Black Professional Firefighters, Donald Day . . . spoke at the second meeting. . . . Day contrasted New Haven's experience with that of nearby Bridgeport, where minority firefighters held one-third of lieutenant and captain positions. Bridgeport, Day observed, had once used a testing process similar to New Haven's, with a written exam accounting for 70 percent of an applicant's score, an oral exam for 25 percent, and seniority for the remaining five percent. Bridgeport recognized, however, that the oral component, more so than the written component, addressed the sort of "real-life scenarios" fire officers encounter on the job.

Accordingly, that city "changed the relative weights" to give primacy to the oral exam. Since that time, Day reported, Bridgeport had seen minorities "fairly represented" in its exam results. . . .

At its fourth meeting, CSB solicited the views of three individuals with testing-related expertise. Dr. Christopher Hornick, an industrial/organizational psychology consultant with 25 years' experience with police and firefighter testing, described the exam results as having "relatively high adverse impact." . . . [H]e advised the CSB, to consider "the broader issue of how your procedures and your rules and the types of tests that you are using are contributing to the adverse impact." . . .

Hornick described the written test itself as "reasonably good," but he criticized the decision not to allow Department officials to check the content. According to Hornick, this "inevitably" led to "test[ing] for processes and procedures that don't necessarily match up into the department." . . .

. . . Vincent Lewis, a specialist with the Department of Homeland Security and former fire officer in Michigan . . . . urged the CSB to consider whether candidates had, in fact, enjoyed equal access to the study materials.

Janet Helms, a professor of counseling psychology at Boston College, observed that two-thirds of the incumbent fire officers who submitted job analyses to IOS during the exam design phase were Caucasian. Members of different racial groups, Helms told the CSB, sometimes do their jobs in different ways, "often because the experiences that are open to white male firefighters are not open to members of these other under-represented groups." The heavy reliance on job analyses from white firefighters, she suggested, may thus have introduced an element of bias.

The CSB's fifth and final meeting began with statements from City officials recommending against certification. New Haven's counsel, repeated the applicable disparate-impact standard:

> "[A] finding of adverse impact is the beginning, not the end, of a review of testing procedures. Where a procedure demonstrates adverse impact, you look to how closely it is related to the job that you're looking to fill and you also look at whether there are other ways to test for those qualities, those traits, those positions that are equally valid with less adverse impact."

New Haven, . . . other officials asserted, would be vulnerable to Title VII liability under this standard. . . .

After giving members of the public a final chance to weigh in, the CSB voted on certification, dividing 2 to 2. By rule, the result was noncertification. . . .

## C

Following the CSB's vote, petitioners—17 white firefighters and one Hispanic firefighter, all of whom had high marks on the exams—filed suit in the United States District Court for the District of Connecticut. . . . By opposing certification, petitioners alleged, respondents had discriminated against them in violation of Title VII's disparate-treatment provision and the Fourteenth Amendment's Equal Protection Clause. The decision not to certify, respondents answered, was a lawful effort to comply with Title VII's disparate-impact provision and thus could not have run afoul of Title VII's prohibition of disparate treatment . . .

# II

## A

Title VII became effective in July 1965. Employers responded to the law by eliminating rules and practices that explicitly barred racial minorities from "white" jobs. But removing overtly race-based job classifications did not usher in genuinely equal opportunity. More subtle—and sometimes unconscious— forms of discrimination replaced once undisguised restrictions. . . .

In response to . . . "a number of . . . recent decisions by the United States Supreme Court that sharply cut back on the scope and effectiveness of [civil rights] laws," Congress enacted the Civil Rights Act of 1991. Among the 1991 alterations, Congress formally codified the disparate-impact component of Title VII. . . . Once a complaining party demonstrates that an employment practice causes a disparate impact, amended Title VII states, the burden is on the employer "to demonstrate that the challenged practice is job related for the position in question and consistent with business necessity." . . .

## B . . .

. . . [T]he Court today sets at odds the statute's core directives. When an employer changes an employment practice in an effort to comply with Title VII's disparate-impact provision, the Court reasons, it acts "because of race"—something Title VII's disparate-treatment provision generally forbids. This characterization of an employer's compliance-directed action shows little attention to Congress' design . . .

. . . Congress declared unambiguously that selection criteria operating to the disadvantage of minority group members can be retained only if justified by business necessity. In keeping with Congress' design, employers who reject such criteria due to reasonable doubts about their reliability can hardly be held to have engaged in discrimination "because of" race. A reasonable endeavor to comply with the law and to ensure that qualified candidates of all races have a fair opportunity to compete is simply not what Congress meant to interdict. . . .

## C

To "reconcile" the supposed "conflict" between disparate treatment and disparate impact, the Court offers an enigmatic standard. Employers may attempt to comply with Title VII's disparate-impact provision, the Court declares, only where there is a "strong basis in evidence" documenting the necessity of their action. The Court's standard, drawn from inapposite equal protection precedents, is not elaborated. One is left to wonder what cases would meet the standard and why the Court is so sure this case does not. . . .

# III

## A

. . . I would hold that New Haven had ample cause to believe its selection process was flawed and not justified by business necessity. . . . [P]etitioners have not shown that New Haven's failure to certify the exam results violated Title VII's disparate-treatment provision.

The City, all agree, "was faced with a prima facie case of disparate-impact liability . . ." Its investigation revealed grave cause for concern about the exam process itself and the City's failure to consider alternative selection devices.

Relying heavily on written tests to select fire officers is a questionable practice, to say the least. Successful fire officers, the City's description of the position makes clear, must have the "[a]bility to lead personnel effectively, maintain discipline, promote harmony, exercise sound judgment, and cooperate with other officials." These qualities are not well measured by written tests. . . .

. . . [I]t is unsurprising that most municipal employers do not evaluate their fire-officer candidates as New Haven does. Although comprehensive statistics are scarce, a 1996 study found that nearly two-thirds of surveyed municipalities used assessment centers ("simulations of the real world of work") as part of their promotion processes. . . .

Testimony before the CSB indicated that these alternative methods were both more reliable and notably less discriminatory in operation. . . . Considering the prevalence of these proven alternatives, New Haven was poorly positioned to argue that promotions based on its outmoded and exclusionary selection process qualified as a business necessity. . . .

. . . [T]he City had other reasons to worry about its vulnerability to disparate-impact liability. . . . Testimony before the CSB . . . raised questions concerning unequal access to study materials, and the potential bias introduced by relying principally on job analyses from nonminority fire officers to develop the exams.

In sum, the record solidly establishes that the City had good cause to fear disparate-impact liability. Moreover, the

Court supplies no tenable explanation why the evidence of the tests' multiple deficiencies does not create at least a triable issue under a strong-basis-in-evidence standard.

## B

Concurring in the Court's opinion, Justice Alito asserts that . . . [a] reasonable jury . . . could have found that respondents were not actually motivated by concern about disparate-impact litigation, but instead sought only "to placate a politically important [African-American] constituency." . . .

. . . Justice Alito's analysis contains a more fundamental flaw: It equates political considerations with unlawful discrimination. . . . That political officials would have politics in mind is hardly extraordinary, and there are many ways in which a politician can attempt to win over a constituency—including a racial constituency—without engaging in unlawful discrimination. As courts have recognized, "[p]oliticians routinely respond to bad press . . . , but it is not a violation of Title VII to take advantage of a situation to gain political favor."

. . . It is indeed regrettable that the City's noncertification decision would have required all candidates to go through another selection process. But it would have been more regrettable to rely on flawed exams to shut out candidates who may well have the command presence and other qualities needed to excel as fire officers. Yet that is the choice the Court makes today. It is a choice that breaks the promise of *Griggs* that groups long denied equal opportunity would not be held back by tests "fair in form, but discriminatory in operation."

═══

This case presents an unfortunate situation, one New Haven might well have avoided had it utilized a better selection process in the first place. But what this case does not present is race-based discrimination in violation of Title VII. I dissent from the Court's judgment, which rests on the false premise that respondents showed "a significant statistical disparity," but "nothing more."

# Dissenting Opinion in
# *Shelby County v. Holder* (2013)

*Among the most monumental laws passed in American history is the Voting Rights Act of 1965. Written in response to widespread obstacles keeping African American people from the polls, the act included a provision requiring certain specified jurisdictions with a history of discriminatory voting practices to "preclear" any changes to voting laws with the federal Department of Justice. After more than fifty years of that provision being in effect, a group in Shelby County, Alabama—one of the regions subject to preclearance—challenged the constitutionality of the preclearance provisions. The Supreme Court agreed in large part with the challenge to the law, striking down the preclearance formula as outdated and unrelated to present discrimination. Justice Ginsburg's dissent stands as a moving tribute to the original purpose of the law while explaining how the preclearance provisions are a legal and effective vehicle for realizing the Fourteenth Amendment's promise of equal protection and the Fifteenth Amendment's promise of equal access to voting.*

# I

"[V]oting discrimination still exists; no one doubts that." But the Court today terminates the remedy that proved to be best suited to block that discrimination. The Voting Rights Act of 1965 (VRA) has worked to combat voting discrimination where other remedies had been tried and failed. Particularly effective is the VRA's requirement of federal preclearance for all changes to voting laws in the regions of the country with the most aggravated records of rank discrimination against minority voting rights.

A century after the Fourteenth and Fifteenth Amendments guaranteed citizens the right to vote free of discrimination on the basis of race, the "blight of racial discrimination in voting" continued to "infec[t] the electoral process in parts of our country." Early attempts to cope with this vile infection resembled battling the Hydra. Whenever one form of voting discrimination was identified and prohibited, others sprang up in its place. This Court repeatedly encountered the remarkable "variety and persistence" of laws disenfranchising minority citizens. . . .

. . . [T]he Voting Rights Act became one of the most consequential, efficacious, and amply justified exercises of federal legislative power in our Nation's history. Requiring federal preclearance of changes in voting laws in the covered jurisdictions—those States and localities where opposition to the Constitution's commands were most virulent—the VRA provided a fit solution for minority voters as well as for States. Under the preclearance regime established by §5 of the VRA, covered jurisdictions must submit proposed changes in voting laws or procedures to the Department of Justice (DOJ), which has 60 days to respond to the changes. A change will be approved unless DOJ finds it has "the purpose [or] . . . the effect of denying or abridging the right to vote on account of race or color." . . .

After a century's failure to fulfill the promise of the Fourteenth and Fifteenth Amendments, passage of the VRA finally led to signal improvement on this front. "The Justice Department estimated that in the five years after [the VRA's] passage, almost as many blacks registered [to vote] in Alabama, Mississippi, Georgia, Louisiana, North Carolina, and South Carolina as in the entire century before 1965." And in assessing the overall effects of the VRA in 2006, Congress found that "[s]ignificant progress has been made in eliminating first generation barriers experienced by minority voters, including increased numbers of registered minority voters, minority voter turnout, and minority representation in Congress, State legislatures, and local elected offices. This progress is the direct result of the Voting Rights Act of 1965." On that matter of cause and effects there can be no genuine doubt. . . .

. . . Congress reauthorized the VRA for five years in 1970, for seven years in 1975, and for 25 years in 1982. Each time, this Court upheld the reauthorization as a valid exercise of congressional power. As the 1982 reauthorization approached its 2007 expiration date, Congress again considered whether the VRA's preclearance mechanism remained an appropriate response to the problem of voting discrimination in covered jurisdictions.

Congress did not take this task lightly. Quite the opposite. The 109th Congress that took responsibility for the renewal started early and conscientiously. . . . In mid-July, the House . . . passed the reauthorization by a vote of 390 yeas to 33 nays. The bill was read and debated in the Senate, where it passed by a vote of 98 to 0. President Bush signed it a week later, on July 27, 2006, recognizing the need for "further work . . . in the fight against injustice," and calling the reauthorization "an example of our continued commitment to a united America where every person is valued and treated with dignity and respect."

In the long course of the legislative process, Congress "amassed a sizable record." . . .

After considering the full legislative record, Congress made the following findings: The VRA has directly caused significant progress in eliminating first-generation barriers to ballot access, leading to a marked increase in minority voter registration and turnout and the number of minority elected officials. But despite this progress, "second generation barriers constructed to prevent minority voters from fully participating in the electoral process" continued to exist, as well as racially polarized voting in the covered jurisdictions, which increased the political vulnerability of racial and language minorities in those jurisdictions. Extensive "[e]vidence of continued discrimination," Congress concluded, "clearly show[ed] the continued need for Federal oversight" in covered jurisdictions. The overall record demonstrated to the federal lawmakers that, "without the continuation of the Voting Rights Act of 1965 protections, racial and language minority citizens will be deprived of the opportunity to exercise their right to vote, or will have their votes diluted, undermining the significant gains made by minorities in the last 40 years."

Based on these findings, Congress reauthorized preclearance for another 25 years, while also undertaking to reconsider the extension after 15 years to ensure that the provision was still necessary and effective. The question before the Court is whether Congress had the authority under the Constitution to act as it did.

# II

In answering this question, the Court does not write on a clean slate. It is well established that Congress' judgment regarding exercise of its power to enforce the Fourteenth and Fifteenth Amendments warrants substantial deference. The VRA addresses the combination of race discrimination and the right to vote, which is "preservative of all rights." When confronting the most constitutionally invidious form of discrimination, and the most fundamental right in our democratic system, Congress' power to act is at its height.

The basis for this deference is firmly rooted in both constitutional text and precedent. The Fifteenth Amendment, which targets precisely and only racial discrimination in voting rights, states that, in this domain, "Congress shall have power to enforce this article by appropriate legislation." In choosing this language, the Amendment's framers invoked Chief Justice Marshall's formulation of the scope of Congress' powers under the Necessary and Proper Clause:

> "Let the end be legitimate, let it be within the scope of the constitution, and *all means which are appropriate, which are plainly adapted to that end*, which are not prohibited, but consist with the letter and spirit of the constitution, are constitutional."

It cannot tenably be maintained that the VRA, an Act of Congress adopted to shield the right to vote from racial discrimination, is inconsistent with the letter or spirit of the Fifteenth Amendment, or any provision of the Constitution read in light of the Civil War Amendments. Nowhere in today's opinion, . . . is there clear recognition of the transformative effect the Fifteenth Amendment aimed to achieve. . . .

# III

## A

I begin with the evidence on which Congress based its decision to continue the preclearance remedy. The surest way to evaluate whether that remedy remains in order is to see if preclearance is still effectively preventing discriminatory changes to voting laws. . . .

All told, between 1982 and 2006, DOJ objections blocked over 700 voting changes based on a determination that the changes were discriminatory. Congress found that the majority of DOJ objections included findings of discriminatory intent, and that the changes blocked by preclearance were "calculated decisions to keep minority voters from fully participating in the political process." On top of that, over the same time period the DOJ and private plaintiffs succeeded in more than 100 actions to enforce the §5 preclearance requirements. . . .

. . . Surveying the type of changes stopped by the preclearance procedure conveys a sense of the extent to which §5 continues to protect minority voting rights. Set out below are characteristic examples of changes blocked in the years leading up to the 2006 reauthorization:

- In 1995, Mississippi sought to reenact a dual voter registration system, "which was initially enacted in 1892 to disenfranchise Black voters," and for that reason, was struck down by a federal court in 1987. . . .

• In 2004, Waller County, Texas, threatened to prosecute two black students after they announced their intention to run for office. The county then attempted to reduce the availability of early voting in that election at polling places near a historically black university. . . .

These examples, and scores more like them, fill the pages of the legislative record. The evidence was indeed sufficient to support Congress' conclusion that "racial discrimination in voting in covered jurisdictions [remained] serious and pervasive."

Congress further received evidence indicating that formal requests of the kind set out above represented only the tip of the iceberg. . . . This evidence gave Congress ever more reason to conclude that the time had not yet come for relaxed vigilance against the scourge of race discrimination in voting.

True, conditions in the South have impressively improved since passage of the Voting Rights Act. Congress noted this improvement and found that the VRA was the driving force behind it. But Congress also found that voting discrimination had evolved into subtler second-generation barriers, and that eliminating preclearance would risk loss of the gains that had been made. Concerns of this order, the Court previously found, gave Congress adequate cause to reauthorize the VRA. . . .

### B

I turn next to the evidence on which Congress based its decision to reauthorize the coverage formula in §4(b). Because Congress did not alter the coverage formula, the same jurisdictions previously subject to preclearance continue to be covered by this remedy. . . .

There is no question . . . that the covered jurisdictions have a unique history of problems with racial discrimination in voting. . . . The Court criticizes Congress for failing to recognize that "history did not end in 1965." But the Court ignores that "what's past is prologue." And "[t]hose who cannot remember the past are condemned to repeat it." Congress was especially mindful of the need to reinforce the gains already made and to prevent backsliding.

Of particular importance, even after 40 years and thousands of discriminatory changes blocked by preclearance, conditions in the covered jurisdictions demonstrated that the formula was still justified by "current needs."

Congress learned of these conditions through a report, known as the Katz study, that looked at §2 suits between 1982 and 2004. . . . The study's findings . . . indicated that racial discrimination in voting remains "concentrated in the jurisdictions singled out for preclearance." . . .

. . . Congress might have been charged with rigidity had it afforded covered jurisdictions no way out or ignored jurisdictions that needed superintendence. Congress, however, responded to this concern. Critical components of the congressional design are the statutory provisions allowing jurisdictions to "bail out" of preclearance, and for court-ordered "bail ins." . . .

Congress was satisfied that the VRA's bailout mechanism provided an effective means of adjusting the VRA's coverage over time. . . . Nearly 200 jurisdictions have successfully bailed out of the preclearance requirement, and DOJ has consented to every bailout application filed by an eligible jurisdiction since the current bailout procedure became effective in 1984. The bail-in mechanism has also worked. . . .

This experience exposes the inaccuracy of the Court's portrayal of the Act as static, unchanged since 1965. Congress designed the VRA to be a dynamic statute, capable of adjusting to changing conditions. . . .

## IV

Congress approached the 2006 reauthorization of the VRA with great care and seriousness. The same cannot be said of the Court's opinion today. The Court makes no genuine attempt to engage with the massive legislative record that Congress assembled. Instead, it relies on increases in voter registration and turnout as if that were the whole story. Without even identifying a standard of review, the Court dismissively brushes off arguments based on "data from the record," and declines to enter the "debat[e about] what [the] record shows." One would expect more from an opinion striking at the heart of the Nation's signal piece of civil-rights legislation.

I note the most disturbing lapses. First, by what right, given its usual restraint, does the Court even address Shelby County's facial challenge to the VRA? . . . Third, hardly showing the respect ordinarily paid when Congress acts to implement the Civil War Amendments, and as just stressed, the Court does not even deign to grapple with the legislative record.

## A

Shelby County launched a purely facial challenge to the VRA's 2006 reauthorization. "A facial challenge to a legislative Act," the Court has other times said, "is, of course, the most difficult challenge to mount successfully, since the challenger must establish that no set of circumstances exists under which the Act would be valid."

. . . Yet the Court's opinion in this case contains not a word explaining why Congress lacks the power to subject to preclearance the particular plaintiff that initiated this lawsuit—Shelby County, Alabama. The reason for the Court's silence is apparent, for as applied to Shelby County, the VRA's preclearance requirement is hardly contestable. . . .

. . . Although circumstances in Alabama have changed, serious concerns remain. Between 1982 and 2005, . . . even while subject to the restraining effect of §5, Alabama was found to have "deni[ed] or abridge[d]" voting rights "on account of race or color" more frequently than nearly all other States in the Union. . . . Alabama's sorry history of §2 violations alone provides sufficient justification for Congress' determination in 2006 that the State should remain subject to §5's preclearance requirement. . . .

A recent FBI investigation provides a further window into the persistence of racial discrimination in state politics. Recording devices worn by state legislators cooperating with the FBI's investigation captured conversations between members of the state legislature and their political allies. The recorded conversations are shocking. Members of the state Senate derisively refer to African-Americans as "Aborigines" and talk openly of their aim to quash a particular gambling-related referendum because the referendum, if placed on the ballot, might increase African-American voter turnout. . . . These conversations occurred not in the 1870's, or even in the 1960's, they took place in 2010. . . .

These recent episodes forcefully demonstrate that §5's preclearance requirement is constitutional as applied to Alabama and its political subdivisions. And under our case law, that conclusion should suffice to resolve this case. . . .

## C

The Court has time and again declined to upset legislation of this genre unless there was no or almost no evidence of unconstitutional action by States. . . . No such claim can be made about the congressional record for the 2006 VRA reauthorization. Given a record replete with examples of denial or abridgment of a paramount federal right, the Court should have left the matter where it belongs: in Congress' bailiwick.

Instead, the Court strikes §4(b) 's coverage provision because, in its view, the provision is not based on "current conditions." . . . Volumes of evidence supported Congress' determination that the prospect of retrogression was real. Throwing out preclearance when it has worked and is continuing to work to stop discriminatory changes is like throwing away your umbrella in a rainstorm because you are not getting wet.

But, the Court insists, the coverage formula is no good; it is based on "decades-old data and eradicated practices." Even if the legislative record shows, as engaging with it would reveal, that the formula accurately identifies the jurisdictions with the worst conditions of voting discrimination, that is of no moment, as the Court sees it. Congress, the Court decrees, must "star[t] from scratch." I do not see why that should be so. . . .

The sad irony of today's decision lies in its utter failure to grasp why the VRA has proven effective. The Court appears to believe that the VRA's success in eliminating the specific devices extant in 1965 means that preclearance is no longer needed. With that belief, and the argument derived from it, history repeats itself. The same assumption—that the problem could be solved when particular methods of voting discrimination are identified and eliminated—was indulged and proved wrong repeatedly prior to the VRA's enactment. Unlike prior statutes, which singled out particular tests or devices, the VRA is grounded in Congress' recognition of the "variety and persistence" of measures designed to impair minority voting rights. In truth, the evolution of voting discrimination into more subtle second-generation barriers is powerful evidence that a remedy as effective as preclearance remains vital to protect minority voting rights and prevent backsliding.

Beyond question, the VRA is no ordinary legislation. It is extraordinary because Congress embarked on a mission long delayed and of extraordinary importance: to realize the purpose and promise of the Fifteenth Amendment. For a half century, a concerted effort has been made to end racial discrimination in voting. Thanks to the Voting Rights Act, progress once the subject of a dream has been achieved and continues to be made.

The record supporting the 2006 reauthorization of the VRA is also extraordinary. It was described by the Chairman of the House Judiciary Committee as "one of the most extensive considerations of any piece of legislation that the United States Congress has dealt with in the 27½ years" he had served in the House. After exhaustive evidence-gathering and deliberative process, Congress reauthorized the VRA, including the coverage provision, with overwhelming bipartisan support. It was the judgment of Congress that "40 years has not been a sufficient amount of time to eliminate the vestiges of discrimination following nearly 100 years of disregard for the dictates of the 15th amendment and to ensure that the right of all citizens to vote is protected as guaranteed by the Constitution." That determination of the body empowered to enforce the Civil War Amendments "by appropriate legislation" merits this Court's utmost respect. In my judgment, the Court errs egregiously by overriding Congress' decision.

———

For the reasons stated, I would affirm the judgment of the Court of Appeals.

# Acknowledgments

I would like to thank all of the people who have helped bring this series to life by reading drafts, providing edits, and helping to put together the final versions. Aidan Calvelli provided careful editing and thoughtful input on all aspects of the series. Priyanka Podugu brought a keen eye to helping me compile materials, highlighting selections that brought out the key themes of liberty. My wife, Allison Brettschneider, was, as she always is, an invaluable partner in this work, giving substantive editorial feedback. David McNamee, Kevin McGravey, Megan Bird, Olivia Siemens, Amistad Meeks, Noah Klein, and Rakhi Kundra all graciously read drafts and provided valuable comments and suggestions. I would also like to thank Elda Rotor and Elizabeth Vogt from Penguin for all they have done to make this series possible, and Rafe Sagelyn, my agent, for his continued support, encouragement, and guidance.

# Unabridged Source Materials

Brief for the Appellant, *Reed v. Reed*, 404 U.S. 71 (1971).

Brief of the American Civil Liberties Union, *Amicus Curiae*, in *Craig v. Boren*, 429 U.S. 190 (1976).

*Ledbetter v. Goodyear Tire and Rubber Co., Inc.*, 550 U.S. 618 (2007) (Ginsburg, J., Dissenting).

*United States v. Virginia*, 518 U.S. 515 (1996).

Brief for the Petitioner, *Struck v. Secretary of Def.*, 409 U.S. 1071 (1972) (No. 72–178), 1972 WL 135840.

*Gonzales v. Carhart*, 550 U.S. 124 (2007) (Ginsburg, J., Dissenting).

*Burwell v. Hobby Lobby Stores, Inc.*, 573 U.S. __ (2014) (Ginsburg, J., Dissenting).

*Whole Woman's Health v. Hellerstedt*, 579 U.S. __ (2016) (Ginsburg, J., Concurring).

*Adarand Constructors, Inc. v. Peña*, 515 U.S. 200 (1995) (Ginsburg, J., Dissenting).

*Olmstead v. L.C.*, 527 U.S. 581 (1999).

*Bush v. Gore*, 531 U.S. 98 (2000) (Ginsburg, J., Dissenting).

*Ricci v. DeStefano*, 557 U.S. __ (2009) (Ginsburg, J., Dissenting).

*Shelby County v. Holder*, 570 US 529 (2013) (Ginsburg, J., Dissenting).